FIGHT

LIKE A *Girl*

⸺◦◦◦⸺

MY BATTLE WITH ALS

Lesley Krummel

ISBN 978-1-0980-0916-8 (paperback)
ISBN 978-1-0980-0917-5 (digital)

Christian Faith Publishing, Inc.
832 Park Avenue
Meadville, PA 16335
www.christianfaithpublishing.com

Printed in the United States of America

I dedicate this book to my wonderful family. My loving and supportive husband, my beautiful children, and the lights of my life, my grandchildren. I could not have kept going without all of you. And I want to thank my mom for always being here for me. Love you all!

Contents

Acknowledgments

Before I was diagnosed with ALS, I would have never thought about writing. But it seemed like after I found out that I had this awful, nasty, degrading, life-changing disease, I have had the urge to write. If I haven't sat down and written for a while, I just get the urge to do so. And I am positive it is because it is what God has called me to do. So I want to thank God for all He has done for me and for giving me the strength to travel on this ALS journey. I have learned so much and have grown in many different ways. Thanks be to God!

Introduction

I have always been a very active person. I am a fitness instructor at the local YMCA, where I instruct a class called "bodypump." We workout with barbells and free weights. We do one thousand reps in one hour. I have always loved working out.

In January of 2017, things started to change. My balance was off ever so slightly. Things started to feel just a little bit heavier. I had been to Aruba recently, so I thought maybe I had caught a bug. A visit to the doctor and some blood work confirmed that this wasn't the case.

I went about my normal activity for the next several months. As time went by, I was still feeling weaker, and my balance was still off. One other thing that I noticed was the extreme fatigue I was experiencing. It is very hard to describe just how tired I really felt.

By August of 2017, I noticed twitching in my right thigh. I could see them but couldn't feel them. I was a little shocked and scared. I had never noticed my muscles doing this before. I had a neurological appointment coming up in October, so I decided to just wait until then to talk to my doctor about this.

I finally had my appointment and discussed the twitches with my doctor. He didn't seem very concerned and informed me that much of the population experiences muscle twitches at one time or another. That really didn't make me feel any better. I was just concerned about *my* muscle twitches.

Halloween came, and I had my first round of testing. Over the next seven months, I would have lots of blood work done, several EMGs, a lumbar puncture, an EKG, more blood work, several

MRIs, reflex, lung capacity and strength tests, X-rays, and other tests that I am probably forgetting to mention.

The first EMG results came back abnormal. The doctor's impression on the bottom of the report said, "Motor neuron disease cannot be excluded." Wow! That hit me like a ton of bricks. I had thought that maybe that was what was going on with my body, but to see it in print was quite a shock. On May 15, 2018, I was diagnosed with ALS.

I decided to form a closed group on Facebook. Just something for mental and spiritual support from others. It was also a convenient way to keep friends and family updated on my medical appointments and test results.

What happened totally caught me off guard. My little group started growing. Friends were adding friends to the group. People were messaging me, asking me to be a part of the group. And to my surprise, my Faith and Friends group members were commenting on my page of how inspiring the posts were—how uplifting my posts were to them. I knew right away there was something bigger going on. God was using me to speak to others.

I would like to share some of the posts from my Faith and Friends pages. I hope they will inspire and uplift you as well.

Idol

This is the day the Lord hath made. We will rejoice and be glad in it.
—Psalm 118:24

Good morning! I had just finished exercising, which I do most every day and have for the last thirty-five years faithfully. It is getting harder and harder. I used to be able to do crunches, planks, push-ups—you name it, and I could do them forever. I love to lift weights. I love "body-pump" and any kind of weight training. I still do these things even though I have had to cut back and gave up instructing at the YMCA in Atlantic, Iowa. That broke my heart! It is just getting harder and harder.

I also love to do Zumba-type workouts. A group of friends and I get together three mornings a week to work out. I have self-taught myself Zumba-type workouts. I got voted to be the leader since I had the experience instructing. Of course, I can't really jump anymore, but I move around the best I can. We have a blast.

I was thinking about how much weight I used to able to lift, how strong my core was, I could do tons of reps, and my endurance was great. Now, I really have to watch what I do because if I break down my muscle, it won't build back up. I am losing muscle, and I can't do anything about it. I have been working on toning and strengthening my muscles for years; now, I can see them and feel them slipping away.

I was driving home the other day, and I heard the word "idol" plain and clear.

"What do I mean then? That a thing sacrificed to idols, is anything, or that an idol is anything" (1 Corinthians 10:19)?

So basically, if I spend all of my time thinking about or worrying about how I can't do what I used to be able to do or worry about losing my strength or muscle tone, I am making that an idol. God clearly says not to make idols. We are to give everything to Him. I think that is what is getting me through this journey of finding out that I have ALS. It is scary not knowing what is going to happen or what to expect. So I am giving it to God. I am trying not to worry or be scared.

"Be careful for nothing; but in everything by prayer and supplication with thanksgiving let our requests be made known to God" (Philippians 4:6).

Fear is another type of an idol. We can't be afraid to step out in faith. God wants us to trust Him and give all our fears and failures to Him. I am trying to remember that and try to remember that I am not in control. I am not. So as Mandisa says in her song, "Overcomer," I will stay in this fight till the very end. And in her song "Unfinished," God is not finished with me yet. Mandisa is a very smart woman! Have a wonderful day!

Endure

*Consider it pure joy, brothers and sisters, whenever
you face trials of many kinds, because you know that
the testing of your faith produces perseverance.*

—James 1:2–3

*W*ell, that really hits home for me. I keep thinking there is definitely something bigger going on here than I or anyone else realizes. The last few days, I keep thinking of the word "endure."

I have problems with my toes. I stub them constantly. It started last summer. It is so bad that I had a friend tell me that he looked online to see if they made "steel-toed" flip-flops. And guess what? They do!

My right foot doesn't want to lift up when I take a step. This results in my big toe bending downward and then getting stepped on. Believe me, this does not feel good! It has happened so often that I don't even yell or scream anymore. I just stop, wait a few minutes for the pain to subside, and then, I go on my way. The toe usually ends up turning a deep shade of purple.

It happened again the other day as I was walking through our yard. But my first thought was, *I will persevere! I know, Mom, I should just wear shoes instead of flip-flops, but it's summer!* I know that God has big plans for me, so I will just push through this and persevere.

I love music, and contemporary Christian music is one of my favorites. One of the most amazing artists is Amy Grant. She has a new song out called "More than Anything." Some of the words in the song are, "I know if You wanted to, You could wave Your hand.

Spare me this heartache and change Your plan. I know any second, You could take my pain away. But even if You don't, I pray. You know more than anyone that my flesh is weak. And You know I'd give anything for a remedy. And I'll ask a thousand times more to set me free today. But even if you don't, I pray."

What awesome words! Just remember, we can endure anything with God right beside us. There is a reason we are going through the trials we are in, and someday, we will know why.

"You need to persevere so that when you have done the will of God, you will receive what He has promised" (Hebrews 10:36).

Fishers of Men

"*I* will make you fishers of men, fishers of men, fishers of men. I will make you fishers of men, if you follow me." This is one of the Sunday-school songs that my children sang years ago when they were young. For some reason, I woke up with this song in my head.

The moms of the children attending Sunday school would take turns teaching classes on Sunday mornings. The other Sundays when we weren't teaching class, we would sit and fellowship together while we waited for the kids to get done.

I didn't realize it then how important that time was spent with the other moms. We take for granted what is right in front of our faces. We don't think that it is very important. Then, thirty years later, we look back and think, *Wow, that was a very valuable time in my life!*

As fishers of men, we are to spread the Good News. We are to be a light to those who are caught in the darkness. To be a Christian is to spread the Word of the Lord to give others the privilege that we have experienced which is to be a child of God.

Being a Sunday-school teacher, helping with Bible school, being a song leader in the Alive in Christ choir, and playing in the bell choir have all been opportunities to be a fisher of men. I had never really thought about it before.

I have been blessed to have gone on a mission trip to El Salvador. Never in my life did I think I would ever have the chance to do something like that or even have the guts to go. The opportunity arose, and I knew I wanted to be a part of it. I have made a lifelong friend in a little girl named Paola. We bonded in one week in a way that is hard to explain. We couldn't communicate verbally, so we drew pictures in the dirt. Just by our gestures we could understand each other. I am still able to be in contact with this little girl from El Salvador that stole my heart.

When our outreach group met again after our trip to El Salvador, we decided that we wanted to something for our local communities. We started a clothing pantry. Soon, we were able to add a food pantry. We serve around twenty-five families a week. How blessed are we to belong to a church family that has the resources and the time to be able to do this?

"For we are God's handywork, created in Christ Jesus to do good works which God prepared in advance for us to do" (Ephesians 2:10).

So God knew all along that I would teach Sunday school, go to El Salvador, and be a song leader in our church. I think that God is telling us to remember to spread the Good Word and to be fishers of men. I hear ya, Lord!

Revelations

*W*e are driving the pickup, pulling the pontoon. We are headed north. The radio reception is very sketchy. I was just thinking about how I hadn't heard from God lately. Then, I hear the words come over the radio, "Everybody keeps talking about heaven like they can't wait to go. Everybody keeps talking about how it's gonna be so beautiful."

I have no idea who was singing it; it sounded like a country song. I don't even know if those were the exact words. Then, the radio reception went out again, and I couldn't hear the rest of the song. I think I just heard from God!

Whenever I think about visiting a tropical island, I think about how beautiful it is. But then, I think about heaven. Nothing compares.

"The twelve gates were twelve pearls, each gate made of a single pearl. The great street of the city was gold, as pure as transparent glass" (Revelations 21:21).

Sounds amazing. And we will feel amazing as well.

"He will wipe away every tear from their eyes. There will be no more death or mourning or crying or pain, for the old has passed away" (Revelations 21:4).

Now that will be quite a trip! But right now, I will settle for Okoboji!

Fear

*I*t started at church this morning. Our pastor played the video to the song "Fear Is a Liar." Then, I got into my vehicle to go get groceries and guess what was on the radio? Yep, "Fear Is a Liar." I love that song, so it was fine with me!

While we were on vacation, my husband told me that he had brought an inflatable paddle board for me to use. I was super excited because I had learned to paddleboard in Aruba. The waves were huge there because it is always so windy there. Whenever I would try to stand up and paddle, the wind would blow me backward.

So when Mike told me that he had borrowed one from our friends, I was very excited. Mike steadied me by the dock while I was trying to get my balance on the board. I started paddling away from the dock. If you have ever tried to paddle board, you know that it takes extreme balance and strength in your legs.

My balance is not what it used to be, and my legs are not as strong as they were when I was in Aruba. So I was thrilled that I was able to do it! I fell off one time and was able to pull myself back up onto the board in the water and even stand back up. This may not sound like a big deal, but believe me, it is!

I am so glad I didn't let fear get the best of me. I would have never known that I could still paddleboard.

"Have I not commanded you? Be strong and courageous. Do not be afraid; do not be discouraged, for the Lord your God will be with you wherever you."

Here Comes the Sun

I was driving this morning, and the sun's rays were shining through the clouds and the fog. It was beautiful. Just like a painting. And I thought, *God has been busy again!* Of course, a song came into my head.

"The sun comes up, it's a new day dawning, it's time to sing your song again. Whatever may pass and whatever lies before me, let me be singing when the evening comes." How true is that? No matter what happens, we need to be singing! In other words, look at the bright side, the cup half full, lemonade not lemons, you get the idea. Try to be grateful and blessed for each new day.

We are so blessed to have our children and grandchildren living within a few miles of us. We are able to see them every week. (It doesn't hurt to have a pool, there is a method to my madness!) I never would have dreamed I would have been blessed with such a beautiful family.

I heard something on K-LOVE radio today. Every day, we need to pick someone to pray for. It will make a difference for both of you. Prayers are so powerful! I know I am being prayed for. I can feel it, and so many people have come up to me to tell me they are praying for me, their churches are praying for me, the town is praying for me. How can you not feel that? It is awesome! God is awesome!

"Bless the Lord O my soul; and all that is within me, bless his holy name. Bless the Lord O my soul and forget not all His benefits; who forgiveth all thine iniquities; who healeth all thy diseases; who redeemeth thy life from destruction; who crowneth thee with loving kindness and tender mercies; who satisfieth thy mouth with good things; so that thy youth is renewed like eagles" (Psalms 103:1–5).

Don't Be Discouraged

*T*his morning was a little bit of a reality check for me. I went walking with a group of friends. Whenever I have walked with a group of people, I have had no problem keeping up. In fact, I was usually at the head of the pack. I think I am a little more competitive than I thought!

Today, I could not keep up with them. My legs just wouldn't go any faster. I wasn't out of breath but just couldn't get my legs to move any quicker. It is a very hard thing to accept. But I know there is really nothing I can do about it.

I'm hoping that the ALS clinic in July will be able to work with me and show me things I can do to keep it from progressing and maybe even to help me improve? I'm not going to lie, it really irritates me how long everything takes. I have had to wait and wait throughout this whole process.

My right ankle doesn't bend very well anymore. It is very stiff, and my foot can't bend upward, so I drag my foot sometimes. And I trip and stub my toes a lot too. Ouch! I am a little down today. I got into my vehicle to drive home, and the radio personalities are talking about how God never fails you. He never abandons us. Wow! That is just what I needed to hear. Right at that very moment. It doesn't matter how far I fall behind, He is right there beside me.

"Don't be afraid or discouraged, for the Lord will personally go ahead of you. He will be with you; He will neither fail you nor abandon you" (Deuteronomy 31:8).

I just had an awesome walk with God!

Perfect Timing

I am amazed by God's perfect timing. We think we have it all figured out. We think we know just when something is supposed to happen. And we get very impatient when it doesn't happen in our time. I know I am terrible at waiting. My husband can attest to that! I get an idea in my head, and I am on my way! Sometimes, I may get the cart in front of the horse.

Good things come to those who wait. I'm sure all of you have heard that saying at some time in your lives. I do have to say, most of the time, it is true. I have just experienced this personally. I had hoped for something four years ago. I had located my brother, whom I haven't seen since I was a very young girl, on Facebook. I messaged him, but I got no response. That was really hard for me to stomach. I am one of those people that wants a response very quickly, or it drives me crazy! But I couldn't control this. I just had to let it go.

Yesterday, out of the blue, I got a message from my brother. He hadn't seen my message that I had sent four years ago until today. It really couldn't have been better timing for my brother to respond. Almost like God planned it this way. I'm pretty sure He did! Maybe four years ago wasn't the right time for us to connect.

I ask God, "What is Your timing for my diagnosis?" Why has He picked this time in my life for it to be turned upside down with this diagnosis of ALS? That is where my mind wants to go. But then, I reminded myself, God did not *do* this to me. He is right here by my side, and He knew this was going to happen, but He didn't do it to me. He knows how this will all turn out.

I have no idea how this will all turn out but neither do any of you. None of us knows what our future has in store for us. Unfortunately, I have an idea of what could be coming my way. But as a good friend of mine said, "You have the diagnosis, don't believe the prognosis."

So when I get angry or down, I just think about what my friend said. You know what? It is so true! It may take time, but I am going to be patient and wait for the right time to beat this thing. Maybe, I have a purpose first. Maybe, I am doing genetic testing for a reason. Maybe, I will be able to do some clinical trials that will help to find a cure. Maybe, I will find a stem cell trial to be in. God has perfect timing, not me.

"There is a time for everything, and a season for every activity under the heavens" (Ecclesiastes 3:1).

Forgiveness

I was just thinking about how hard it is to forgive sometimes. Someone may have hurt our feelings. Maybe, they lied to us or talked about us behind our back. They could have started a rumor or left us out of their plans. All these things can hurt our feelings. But have you ever thought about how much energy it takes to stay mad at someone? It weighs you down. It takes tons of energy.

It is also very hard to forgive ourselves for something we may have said or done to someone else. It is actually very hard to forgive someone that we have had an argument with until we forgive ourselves. We must let go and forgive.

"If anyone is in Christ, he is a new creation; old things have passed away; behold all things have become new" (2 Corinthians 5:17).

So basically, if we can't forgive that person and ourselves, we are just throwing God's grace and forgiveness away. I know there was a time I was really upset with someone. I held this hurt and anger in me for years. I finally forgave them, and it was like a weight was lifted off my shoulders. Most of the time, things aren't as bad as we make them out to be. God sacrificed His Son for our sins. We best not take that for granted!

Angels

*A*ngels. I have always been fascinated by angels. While we were at the Creation Museum, there was a room devoted to seven angels. They are Michael (Sunday), Gabriel (Monday), Raphael (Tuesday), Uriel (Wednesday), Selaphiel (Thursday), Raguel (Friday), Barachiel (Saturday). Each angel is related to a weekday. These angels are considered to be high up in the celestial hierarchy. Angels are extensions of God, assisting us and carrying prayers and messages to God.

"For He will command His angels concerning you to guard you in all your ways; on their hands they will bear you up, lest you strike your foot against a stone" (Psalms 91:11–12).

Man, where is my guardian angel when I stub my toe all the time?

Angels are God's servants, carrying out God's will and work for our good.

"Are not all angels ministering spirits sent to serve those who will inherit salvation" (Hebrews 1:14)?

"Do not forget to show hospitality to strangers, for by so doing some people have shown hospitality to angels without knowing it" (Hebrews 13:2).

So quite a while ago, I was at Casey's in Avoca, Iowa. I was getting gas, and I noticed someone across the highway. The person was standing there with several suitcases. The person looked very hot, and I couldn't tell if it was a man or a woman because he or she had so many clothes on, and his or her head was covered up.

I watched this person while my vehicle was filling up with gas. I wondered what he or she was doing. Where is he or she going? I felt bad for the person because he or she was all alone. The gas pump clicked off, and I got out of my vehicle and put the cap back on my gas tank. I pulled out of Casey's slowly because this person was right by the edge of the highway. I looked over and thought it was a woman. I drove past her. And something inside me said, *Stop and help her.*

I am not in the habit of doing this normally. Everything in me said, "Stranger, danger." But before I knew it, I had turned around and stopped behind her. I asked her where she was going, and she said she was heading south down Highway 59. I just happened to be heading to work at our trucking company which was south on 59.

She said she would be happy with a ride to the edge of Avoca. She had several bigger suitcases. I remember thinking, how in the world is she traveling with all these suitcases all by herself?

But I offered to load them up for her. I'm not kidding, they weighed a ton! I could hardly lift them up into my vehicle, and I always considered myself to be pretty strong.

She got into the passenger seat, and I was a little nervous. But we started chatting right away, and she seemed harmless. As we get to the edge of town, I decided to offer her a ride as far as Hancock, Iowa, which is the next town on Highway 59.

She seemed to know the area pretty well. I can't remember her name, but I remember thinking how pretty it was. She asked me questions about my family. How many kids I had, how old were they—things like that.

She just had this calming presence about her. It's hard to explain. As we got closer to Hancock, she asked if I could just take her to Oakland which was the next town after Hancock. I was supposed to be at work, and I would be a little late if I took her, but I agreed to take her.

It was funny because we ended up at Casey's in Oakland. I helped her with her bags and just left her there in front of Casey's. I had the strangest feeling about that encounter. I will never forget what she looked like and her voice. It was very calming. I remember telling my mom what I did, and of course, she wasn't really happy that I had picked up a stranger. But I think she understood after I told her my story. Did I help an angel? Was it a test? I don't know, but part of me wonders if it was. It was all way out of the norm for me, and I haven't felt the urge to pick anyone else up since.

I have one more little story concerning angels. I truly believe that we have guardian angels. There were two separate instances where I'm pretty sure a couple of my grandkids were assisted by their guardian angels.

Both were in situations that could have ended up way worse than they did. They both could have been hurt seriously. The strange thing is, I think they happened at almost the exact same time. But they are both okay. One I witnessed and one I didn't. But they were both very lucky. Or blessed—I think blessed is the right word.

I feel very blessed, as well, to know that God had sent an angel or angels to help and protect me and my family.

"Beware that you do not look down on any of these little ones. For I tell you that in heaven their angels are always in the presence of my heavenly Father" (Matthew 18:10).

Knock and the Door will Be Opened

Ask and it shall be given to you; seek, and you will find; knock, and the door will be opened to you. For everyone who asks shall receive and the one who seeks finds, and to the one who knocks it will be opened.
—Matthew 6:33

Since I had my midline IV put in last week, I have had to cut way back on what I can do. One of those things is to take care of the pool. It is a daily chore. It takes a lot of time and energy to keep it clean.

When we first got the pool, I would ask people that had pools for some tricks of the trade. All of them had the same response: "You will figure it out." Really? That's all you got? I couldn't figure out why they just couldn't tell me when to shock the pool or how much chlorine to use—simple stuff like that. But then, as I went along, I figured out why they wouldn't tell me. No two pools are alike. Everyone has different water; the temperature changes constantly. There are a lot of factors that play into keeping a pool sparkling clean. Who knew?

While I have been out of commission, so to speak, the pool has suffered greatly. Then, we went to Kentucky to the Ark Encounter, and that didn't help the situation. Our son was checking on the pool for us, and he was also doing our livestock chores. He couldn't get the pool figured out. It didn't help that Wanda was broken. Wanda is our automatic pool vacuum—love her! With a lot of time and work, and a new vacuum cleaner, I am getting the pool back in shape. I am now called the "Pool Master!"

I got to thinking how our relationship with God is sort of the same thing. It is a constant process. Sometimes, things are clear;

sometimes, they are a little foggy. God wants us to be constantly seeking Him. God wants us to walk with Him.

We are definitely a work in progress. We are never satisfied with our current state. At least, I don't seem to be. The reason for that is we are unfinished. He really isn't finished with us until the end of our earthly journey. He is molding and using us.

"I love those who love me, and those who seek me diligently find me" (Proverbs 8:17).

Today was day eight out of fourteen for my first set of infusions. It is going very well. I haven't had any side effects and It is getting easier to do them. I am getting the hang of it. I have noticed that I have not had any cramping in my leg at all for a few days! Yay!

Awkward

*H*ave any of you ever found yourself in a very awkward situation and not sure how to handle it? You kind of get that "fight or flight" feeling? Sometimes, we are in these situations before we have time to prevent it. Never a good type of feeling.

Or even if you are just having a bad day, you're feeling down, or things just are not going your way, you wonder, *Why?* Why do these things have to happen to me? I definitely had one of those days today. But I guess what is important is how we handle ourselves in these types of situations.

"Consider it pure joy, my brothers and sisters, whenever you face trials of many kinds; so that you may be mature and complete" (James 1:2, 4).

God is using our troubles to make us stronger. Just like physical exercise, we need spiritual exercise. If our faith is never challenged, our spiritual muscles grow weak. When we have trials or troubles, we are forced to use our spiritual muscles, and then, they grow stronger.

"We know that suffering produces perseverance; perseverance, character; character, hope" (Romans 5:3–4).

The best way to get through these times is to take it to God. Use those spiritual muscles and ask God to help us get through them. This will help us get through anything with grace and to grow in our faith.

Do Not Fear

*T*omorrow is my first ALS clinic. I will be going to UNMC in Omaha, Nebraska. There are only a few ALS clinics across the country, so I feel very thankful that I have one so close.

But I must admit, I am feeling a little anxiety right now. I am so thankful that the appointment is early in the morning, so I don't have to think about it all day.

There will be several appointments all in one day. I will see Dr. T, a physical therapist, occupational, speech, respiratory therapists, and some others that I am not remembering right now.

I am a little concerned as to what or who I will see there. Will there be a lot of other people with ALS there? What stage will they be in? I have asked a couple other ladies that I have come to know because of the common bond of ALS, which is not how you want to meet people, what they thought of the clinics. They both felt it was a very good thing.

It measures your abilities and is a baseline to measure any future progression of the disease. To be honest, I really don't want that thrown in my face. I already have had that experience having gone through about a year's worth of tests. Some tests repeated only to show that, in fact, I have gotten weaker and that the EMG showed more muscle/nerve damage. But this is all necessary for treatment and hopefully for a cure in the future.

The fear of the unknown is getting its grip on me—seriously getting a grip on me. I know that this is not God leaving me, it's the devil trying to get a grip on me. I must stay strong and lean on God. I need to push the devil away.

There have been times in my life that I let the devil trick me; he is very sneaky! But I'm not going to let it happen again. When I let myself get a little down, not sure if I am doing the right things? How do I know if I should be on Radicava or getting an IV port put in? Is this the right move?

I never ever thought I would have to make the decision whether to get a port put in or not. Very scary. It takes me a good two hours each morning to get my infusion done. Is it even helping me? I don't know. It's the fear of the unknown again.

"For God gave us a spirit not of fear, but of power and love and self-control" (Timothy 1:7).

Self-control, interesting. I never thought about it, but self-control is so important yet so hard! But by the grace of God, we have it in us. We just need to use it. We need to take a step back and breathe before we jump to conclusions or react. I know I need to work on this big time! I am trying, I really am.

"Have I not commanded you? Be strong and courageous. Do not be afraid; do not be discouraged for the Lord your God will be with you wherever you go" (Joshua 1:9).

One of my favorite Scriptures. Go out and be strong—be courageous. We can do it!

Kayaking

*Because of the littleness of our faith; for truly I say to you,
if you have the faith the size of a mustard seed, you will
say to this mountain, "Move from here to there," and it
will move, and nothing will be impossible for you.*
—Matthew 17:30

*Y*esterday, a small group of us went kayaking down the Nishnabotna River. A friend and I were talking about how we had wanted to do this, and then, another friend had said she did as well. She asked her sister, and I asked my granddaughter, and we had our group!

I got us all signed up with a guy that has all the kayaks and canoes. Kenna, my granddaughter, and I were going to be in a kayak together. We had discussed, or they told me, "You are going to sit in front because you should be the leader."

I agreed to be the leader and sit in front. So we are ready to get into the kayak and right away, of course, I get into trouble. I'm in mid-air, ready to sit when the guy says, "No, no, no! That isn't how you get in!" Well, I am very committed to the position I was in, so I hurried up and sat down. Kenna got in no problem. The guy then tells us that the person in the *back* is the person in charge. We kind of laughed, and I knew I wasn't going to get back out only to be yelled at again for getting in wrong. I'm sure I would have! We just went with it.

Not two seconds into our maiden voyage, we run into some rocks by the edge of the river, and then, to make it worse, someone else comes and slams into us with their kayak. Okay, maybe slammed is a strong word; maybe bumped is a better one? So we get out of that situation. I am thinking, what did we get ourselves into?

We move out into the river, well, actually, a branch of the river for the first three miles. We are going along, and then, we hear this brushing sound. Pretty soon, we are at a complete stop. Sandbar. The guy had told us about these. But how embarrassing to run into one when he can still see us! He had explained how if you see little ripples, it's the sand under the water. Okay, so two strikes against Kenna and me!

Since Kenna is the leader, she must get out and push us off the sandbar. She did an excellent job. I was thinking, *Man, I'm glad I'm not the leader!* I think we only got stuck on two more sandbars in the eight miles that we went. Not too bad? After that, it was smooth sailing. It was peaceful and beautiful. Kenna even found some old cars sticking out of the banks of the river. You can tell she is from a family of antiquers! Her comment was, "We need to come down here junking!" We enjoyed the view, and some country music, and good conversation. What an awesome afternoon!

When we started out, I had little faith that we were going to be able to pull this off. We even joked about turning around and not getting into the kayak. But we both got more faith as we went along. Just as in life, the tiniest bit of faith, when it is from God, can grow into great proportions, and eventually—hopefully—spread out to the lives of others! Have an awesome day!

Calm

I survived! I cannot tell you all how calm I felt this morning! Unexplainable calm. A 360-degree turnaround from yesterday. I have a sneaky feeling; I know why! It's because of all your prayers, words of support, and comfort! Unbelievable, and of course, it's also because of God.

First of all, I was in a room, and they brought everyone in to me, so I didn't have to go from room to room. Everyone was so nice. I did great on my tests. I got some helpful information and things to consider for the future. I got to do some fun little exercises with my voice. I really can hold a note a lot longer than I thought.

Dr. Thai is the sweetest little guy. He is a very positive, matter-of-fact kind of guy. He looks me right in the eye and says, "I know man who live for long time with ALS. Maybe, after you're around for ten years or so, they say, 'Wrong diagnosis!'" (Did that sound like a Thai accent? Because Dr. T is from Thailand.)

On the way home from the clinic, I dropped everyone off and started down the road to go home, and this song comes on the radio. I love this song.

> Even though I walk through the valley of the shadow of death, Your perfect love is casting out fear. And even when I'm caught in the middle of the storms of this life, I won't turn back, I know you are near. And I will fear no evil, for my God is with me, and if my God is with me, whom then shall I fear, whom then shall I fear?

34

Oh no, You never let go, through the calm and through the storm. Oh no, You never let go, every high and every low. Oh no, You never let go, never let go of me.

I definitely felt His presence today. He was right there with me.

Port Placement

*M*ike and I left the house this morning around 6:00 a.m. I needed to be over at UNMC at 7:00 a.m. We arrived right on time to sit and wait in the lobby, but we weren't late! We are getting pretty good at making it to these appointments on time. Eventually, my name was called, and I get all checked in which is kind of strange because I had already pre-checked in, but I was checked in!

Soon, they came and took me to pre-op. Several nurses and residents came to talk to me and to explain what to expect. One thing that kept being repeated was, "We will give you something to relax you, and then, we will numb you up. This will sting, it will pinch, it will not feel good." I think I was told this like four or five times. Then, one nurse said, "Do you want me to go through what we will be doing, or do you want to be in the dark?"

I said, "I will be in the dark, please!"

Well, to back it up a bit, on the way to the hospital this morning, I remembered someone telling me to just imagine or try to picture Jesus walking right beside you into your appointment. So as I was driving, I was picturing Jesus sitting in the passenger seat. And we are singing karaoke to "Grace Got You" by Mercy Me. It really brought a smile to my face! Jesus is good at karaoke! I always drive with my right hand on the gear shift in the middle of my console, and I'm pretty sure I felt His hand over mine.

So fast forward to me in the operating room. I was lying on the table, and they were prepping me. They had placed a "tent" type cover over my face. This way, I can't see what they were doing. They went over the whole, "We will give you something to relax you, and then we will numb you." I was not going to be "out." I would be awake. They said they would warn me when they started because it will hurt, sting, burn.

I was lying on the table in the operating room, waiting for them to start; I can't see what they were doing. Then, I start to think about what they were doing. I was trying not to cry. I'm pretty sure I had a couple tears. The next thing I know is the "tent" was being pulled away from my face. I looked at the nurses and doctor and asked, "Are you going to stick me pretty soon?" and they kind of chuckled and said, "We are done!"

I couldn't believe it! They said that I was asleep before they were even ready to numb me. They couldn't believe I didn't wake up when they gave me the shot. They didn't knock me out; I was supposed to be awake.

The nurse said, "Yeah, we were talking about '80s bands, we asked you what your favorite bands were, and we looked, and you were out!"

I am still a little amazed at how things went down today. Someone was definitely beside me during this whole process. It was way too easy!

I am sore now, but nothing too terrible. I got the midline out of my arm which is amazing! So anytime you are needing a little extra strength or courage, just remember, Jesus is walking right beside you or singing karaoke with you in your car!

"Fear not, for I am with you; Be not dismayed, for I am your God. I will strengthen you. Yes, I will help you, I will uphold you with My right hand" (Isaiah 41:10).

The War Room

"*I*n order to stand up to the enemy, you need to get on your knees and pray."

This is a quote from one of my favorite movies. "The War Room." You probably wonder what a war room is? Is it a room with all kinds of war memorabilia? Nope. In the movie, a Realtor is showing a house, and in the house is a closet. An elderly lady lives there—Ms. Clara. That is where she goes to pray. To fight everyday battles; to beat the enemy. She also goes there to become closer to God.

Sometimes, we need to go to a nice, quiet place, where we can't be disturbed, to pray and to really talk to God. We need to make space to worship God. Literally. When I first saw this movie, I thought, *Yeah, I'm going to make a war room!* I had good intentions, but I still haven't done it. I really need to get on that! I have a perfect closet for it too!

I started going to Bible study about six years ago. I had never gone before because I had a fear of looking like I had no idea what I was doing. I didn't think I knew the Bible well enough. Everyone else always seemed to know the Bible so well and had Scriptures memorized and knew just how to pray out loud. Praying out loud. That horrified me. I hate to admit it, but it did. I was afraid I would sound so stupid. There is that fear again!

My friend, Shari, who was going to seminary school, asked a few ladies to get together once a month or so. The purpose of this group was supposed to be support for Shari, but as time went on, it quickly became support for those of us who attended as well. At the end of the night, we would go around the room and each of us would pray or add to the prayer. Talk about stage fright! These ladies all sounded so amazing! They were all so good at praying. Not me. Not out loud. I would get all tongue-tied and not know what to say. I wasn't really listening to God or talking to God; I was too worried about what I sounded like to the other ladies. I remember one time, I just ended with, "That's all I got!" I thought to myself, *Did I really just say that?* Now, I know that is not what I was supposed to be doing. I was supposed to be talking to God, not worrying about what I sounded like.

Throughout this process, I'm not kidding you, I witnessed so much growth in one of my friends in particular. I was just amazed. I also learned so much from this group of ladies. And made some lifelong friends.

Before we start exercising in the mornings, our little group makes a circle and prays. We have a couple of ladies that say the prayer. Once again, not all of us are comfortable praying out loud. Sometimes, if both gals are gone, we will say the Lord's Prayer. (Yep, that's what we do Jeanette and Kathy!)

So we don't have to have a war room; we can pray anywhere, anytime. We can pray out loud or just to ourselves, but either way, God can hear us! That's all that matters!

"Rejoice always, pray without ceasing, give thanks in all circumstances; for this is the will of God in Christ Jesus for you" (Thessalonians 5:16–18).

The Rock

*The rain came down, the streams rose, and the winds
blew and beat against that house, yet it did not fall,
because it had its foundation on the rock.*

—Matthew 7:25

*M*ike and I got married very young. I was nineteen, and he was twenty. We both got jobs right out of high school. I drove to Omaha and worked at Mutual of Omaha. Mike worked at a local feed company. We really wanted to start farming, and the only way we could do that was to rent farm ground. Back in the day, whoever rented the farm ground was expected, or were lucky enough, to live in the home that was on the farm. And in our case, we were required to live there in order to farm the ground. Our landlord, Henry, lived in Omaha, and this way, he knew the house was lived in and taken care of.

So just married with no kids, this home was plenty big enough. When we were blessed with three beautiful children, the home seemed to get smaller and smaller. But it was comfortable, and we didn't really have any other options if we wanted to farm the ground. We also raised a lot of hogs throughout those years. Farrow to finish about one thousand head of hogs a year. On dirt. Not cement. I have a lot of stories about those days!

We lived there ten years. An acreage came up for sale a couple towns over. It had a newer ranch-style home, and modern hog facilities, and tons of cement! It was like hog heaven! Sorry, I couldn't help it. We ended up buying this acreage and moving our family. The funny thing is, as small and old as that first house was, it was our home. I remember crying as we were just about ready to drive away for the last time. And believe me, it was nothing to cry over. Except maybe in a happy, joyful way.

So we got moved into our new home. We thought we had it made. We were in heaven. But just because it was a newer home, and had tons of cement, didn't mean things would be easy. A disease went through our hog facility. Something that can't be cured. The only way to get rid of it was to sell everything and clean. And then sit. So basically, our dreams went up in smoke. We couldn't do anything about it. Mike went to work for a trucking company, and I did home daycare. Not anything that we had planned on doing. But we did what we had to do. And we made it. We survived.

I look back at the days in our first home, and all I have are awesome memories. Things were not easy, but man, looking back, we had it all. The reason we had it all was because we had each other, and we had God. We had built our home on a firm foundation. We had built our home on the rock. The rock being Jesus Christ.

As I have talked about before, I went to El Salvador on a mission trip. We went to help build a home for a woman and her mom. They basically lived in a tent. I will never forget when Dora, the daughter, saw her new sink for the first time. They didn't have running water, and she never had a sink. She was getting a very large cement sink. But this sink was very important. It was used for washing clothes, washing dishes, and themselves in. She was so proud of her new sink. She went from a tent made out of plastic, or whatever else she could find, to a home from cinder block. Made me very thankful for what I have.

"Do not let your hearts be troubled. You believe in God; believe also in Me. My Father's house has many rooms; if that were not so, would I have told you that I am going there to prepare a place for you" (John 14:1–2)?

Still, none of these homes will compare to the home our Father is preparing for us. I know, I can't even begin to imagine how beautiful it will be!

Bright Orange Hair?

I was born in Sioux City. I lived on a quiet little dead-end street. It had a cool little turnaround at the end of the street with a big tree in the middle. There was a creek that ran right behind the end of the street that all the neighborhood kids played in, ice skated on, and went over to the other side of the creek where there was a great big hill. Perfect for sledding. We spent hours in that creek. We would head out for our new adventures every day. We would go home for lunch and then head back out. We didn't have cell phones to check in with. We just knew when to go home to check in. When I was a bit older, we moved to another street in that same area. The area was called Leeds. I had a friend that lived across the street. I would be doing dishes after supper, and when I looked out my window, she would be standing outside waiting for me to get done. Evidently, she didn't have to do supper dishes.

One day, we decided to go bike riding. I don't know why, but we were both on my bike. I had a "banana" seat, so we could both fit on it. Well, there were some pretty steep hills on some of those streets. (It's kind of funny when we took our kids back to show them the steep hill, it really didn't look that steep anymore!)

We had the bright idea, or maybe she had the bright idea, that we go down one of the steep hills. I agreed, and we headed down the hill. So I'm in front, steering, and suddenly, I feel the bike kind of weave back-and-forth. I thought, *What is going on?* Then, I can see her arms going up and down like she is flying. Well, we flew, all right! I flew right over the handlebars and slid, basically on my face, down the hill. I remember after the initial shock, I just started screaming.

I had knocked my two front teeth out and some serious road rash, complete with rocks and gravel in my skin.

I looked up, and there was a lady, in her robe with bright orange hair, looking down at me. She was trying to get me to stop screaming. I don't even remember what happened to my friend; I don't think she was hurt as badly. I know there are some lovely photos with me missing my front teeth. But eventually, I got them capped and everything was good again. Until one day, when I decided to eat some taffy and couldn't figure out what the crunchy stuff was in it. Oh, that would be my teeth again. I learned the hard way, you can't eat taffy with capped front teeth!

I guess the reason I am sharing this story, is it just shows that we are going to have ups and downs, but we will always make it through, if we have faith. I am definitely having ups and downs, but we all do. And we are here for each other. That is what God intended for us to do—be here for each other. Even if we are in our robes with bright-orange hair. I seriously wonder what that was all about?

"A new command I give you; Love one another. As I have loved you, so you must love one another. By this everyone will know that you are my disciples, if you love one another" (John 13:34–35).

Life Is a Box of Chocolates

～

"*L*ife is a box of chocolates, you never know what you're going to get" (Forest Gump).

Everyone knows what movie that quote came from. "Forest Gump." I happened to turn the TV on, and it was on. I have seen this movie many times but always seem to take something different away from it each time. Today, it was the part when Forest was on his shrimping boat. He looked toward the docks, and there was Lt. Dan. Lt. Dan had promised if Forest had ever gotten his own shrimping boat, Lt. Dan would become his first mate.

So they take off to find shrimp and can't find any. Lt. Dan tells Forest to take him to his church to pray. Lt. Dan wanted to ask Forest's God to help them find shrimp. Lt. Dan was very skeptical of Forest's God. So they went to church week after week and still no shrimp. Lt. Dan gets very angry with God and asks why. Why isn't he helping them find shrimp?

Pretty soon, a storm comes up out of nowhere, and all the other shrimping boats are crushed against the shore and ruined. All except Forest's boat. So Forest and Lt. Dan catch all the shrimp, since they are the only boat left out there and become wealthy. The best part is Forest used his wealth to help others he had come in contact with in his life that needed help.

There are a couple things I took away from this little snippet from the movie. First, we never know what life is going to bring us. Like a box of chocolates. We can be sailing along, no problem, and then, boom! Things can come crashing down. And second, we need to be persistent with our faith. We can't give up just because God doesn't answer right away. You never know, maybe He is answering in a way we aren't expecting or a way we don't recognize at first. We may get angry and think that God isn't listening when, in fact, He is.

When God answers us, either in a big or small way, we really need to remember to pass on our riches. Not just with our monetary wealth but with our time, talents, and resources. Pay it forward!

And that's all I got to say about that!

Joy

"*I* got the joy, joy, joy, joy down in my heart, down in my heart to stay!"

This is the song I woke up with in my head this morning. The contemporary Christian group, For King and Country, have a new song out called "Joy." It talks about how we need to testify and choose joy. Even with all the bad in the world, get the fire back in your bones! Don't let evil blow it out. Or as the Sunday school song goes, "This little light of mine, I'm gonna let it shine. This little light of mine, I'm going to let it shine, let it shine, let it shine. Don't let satin whoosh it out, I'm gonna let it shine. Don't let satin whoosh it out, I'm gonna let it shine, let it shine, let it shine!"

As you know, I relate to songs a lot. Without music, I would be super sad—and bored! It never fails when I'm driving in my vehicle; a song comes on that fits perfectly with whatever is on my mind at that moment.

With all the scary headlines in the news, it is hard to have joy in your heart. But that is exactly where we need to start. If we don't give in to all the bad news and try to bring more joy into the world, just think what a wonderful world we would live in. Jeesh, I just thought of two songs, "Joy to the World" and "What a Beautiful World." Maybe, I'm not the first one with this novel concept?

"Make a joyful noise unto the Lord, all the earth; and make a loud noise, and rejoice, and sing praise" (Psalm 98:4).

A joyful noise is a bold declaration of God's glorious name and nature. God loves to hear our outward displays of joyful gladness and worship. But fear of what we might look like to others usually keeps us from clapping our hands, singing out loud, or raising our hands to the Lord when we are worshipping in church or anywhere for that matter. But if we are at a football game or a concert, we seem to have no problem doing these things. Weird, huh? Why shouldn't we cheer and clap for our Lord?

"So whatever you eat or drink, or whatever you do, do all to the glory of God" (1 Corinthians 10:31).

Maybe, if we make a conscious decision to bring joy to our day or to others, we could make a small difference in the world. It can't hurt, right? Let's go out and make a joyful noise to the Lord!

Build Each Other Up

"*T*herefore, encourage one another and build one another up, just as you are doing" (Ecclesiastes 4:9–10).

This is exactly what I can say about this group. Totally building each other up!

Back when our kids were in junior high, a group of soccer moms were sitting around, talking. During the conversation, one of the moms says to another, "I used to think that you were a snot."

I was like, "Whoa! Did she really just say that?" Especially since I was the misjudged snot. I guess the key phrase is "used to be." It is funny because by the end of the conversation, I think every one of us had been misjudged at one time or another. Jeesh, I always thought I was pretty nice!

"Judge not, that ye not be judged. For with what judgement ye judge, ye shall be judged: and with what measure ye mete, it shall be measured to you again" (Matthew 7:1–3).

There is a saying, "Be kind for everyone is fighting a hard battle" (Socrates).

How true is that? We have no idea what our neighbor, the clerk at the store, or the guy in the car next to us at a stoplight is going through. I have learned just in the last few weeks, just after my diagnosis, of two people diagnosed with Multiple Sclerosis another diagnosed with non-Hodgkin lymphoma, and another with cancer. All these people live within five miles of me. And I'm guessing that if you met any of us on the street, you would have no idea that any of us were going through our battles.

Alan Alda has just revealed that he has Parkinson's disease. He made the statement that he is not angry; that he actually has a richer life now than before his diagnosis.

I can totally understand where he is coming from. I know, in my case, I have grown in many ways; I think I am appreciating each new day. I am thankful when I wake up in the morning, able to get out of bed. I am blessed to be able to spend more time with my family and friends and to hold my grandbabies. But I think the place in my life I have grown the most is spiritually. I think that this chapter of my life has opened my eyes to what is really important. I have connected with so many people, some of which I haven't really talked to before. God has everything planned out, and He puts people in our lives when we need them.

Let's continue to build each other up and not judge each other. And I really am a very nice person, by the way! We all need to be thankful for our family and friends. Remember, we have no idea what battles each of us are fighting.

Traditions

$\mathcal{F}$amily traditions are very important parts of life. We have several traditions in our family. One of them being going to Okoboji, Iowa, every summer on vacation. I don't know if we have ever missed a summer. It is one thing that we can all depend on and look forward to. Sometimes, we start new traditions like our "Great Amazing Race" at Easter. I make up clues for the teams to find. These clues are all over the town of Walnut. At first, I would give each team the same clues in the same order, but it seemed that some of the teams would make it a little harder for the next team to show up, to find their clues. I finally figured out that it works best to mix the clues up.

Another tradition we had was Christmas Eve at Grandma Hilda's. Grandma Hilda and Grandpa Rhinehart had five children; those five children had eighteen children; those eighteen children had forty-five children. And the family continues to grow.

When Mike and I were first married and started our family, we would get all dressed up and go into Grandma Hilda's house. We would all cram into her comfortable but very small home. We would find a place to sit and not move for fear we would lose our spot. It was basically shoulder to shoulder in there. One year, there were over one hundred people in her home. But none of us minded. We looked forward to it every year. It was tradition.

I remember we would all sing while Mike's mom played the piano. We would eat dinner, and Santa would take a break on his busy night and bring the kids an apple and an orange and peanuts in a paper bag. Then, we would all go to midnight service at Trinity Lutheran Church in Avoca, Iowa. The little kiddos could hardly stay awake. After church, we would head back to Grandma's house. It was midnight. We would have a snack and then head home.

Family traditions are such an important thing. It keeps families in touch as they grow larger, and some of them move away. I know our family members come from near and far for our "Great Amazing Race." All for a traveling golden egg trophy.

Then, there are traditions of the church. There is Sunday school, worship on Sunday mornings, Bible studies, reading of the Scriptures, baptisms, and communion. All these things bring comfort and peace. Oh, yeah, sharing God's peace is another tradition in our church. It takes us quite a while to get that done! We all move around the isles wishing each other peace.

"I appeal to you, brothers and sisters, in the name of our Lord Jesus Christ, that all of you agree with one another in what you say and that there be no divisions among you, but that you be perfectly united in mind and thought" (1 Corinthians 1:10).

God wants us all to live in perfect harmony, so it's important to make every effort to do so to live in peace.

Fortitude

*F*ortitude: Courage in pain and adversity. Synonyms: courage, bravery, moral fiber, strength of mind, strength of character, backbone, true grit, steadfastness.

Have you ever had one of those days or weeks or months that you wish you could just fast forward through and just forget? Nothing seems to be going right? No matter what you do or say, it is wrong? How do we handle those situations?

Sometimes, it is miscommunication between people; sometimes, it is the unwillingness to forgive someone; sometimes, it is not understanding what the other person is going through or has been through. These are all hard things to get through.

"Bear with each other and forgive one another if any of you has a grievance against someone. Forgive as the Lord forgave you. And over all these virtues put on love, which binds them all together in perfect unit" (Colossians 3:13–14).

I know, sometimes, I really don't want to give up on something, no matter how impossible it seems. I just press on, hoping to make a difference and to make everything okay. It doesn't always work. Many things can be working against us. But sometimes, with true grit and steadfastness, we can accomplish these feats.

I have had to make a couple of decisions lately that have been very rough. You weigh out the options. You try to decide what will be best for everyone involved. Sometimes, your heart gets in the way. For me, that is my biggest enemy. I have been told many times, "You have a very big heart." And sometimes, that can work against you. It's hard to believe but true.

The heart can lead us astray in many ways. Some of them are to be in pursuit of material things, to try to fit in with others when we know it isn't in our best interest, and bad choices of what we do in our spare time or recreation and pride. I know I used to have a horrible problem with feeling left out. I wanted to be included. I got my feelings hurt very easily. God has been working in me; it doesn't seem to matter what other people are doing. Most of the time, not all the time, I am human, you know! But I feel I have really gotten a better grip on it now. A big part of that is identifying and admitting your problem and asking God to help you through it. A good friend of mine helped me to see that.

The saying "follow your heart" is very deceiving. It can really get you into trouble!

"He who trusts in his own heart is a fool, but he who walks wisely will be delivered" (Proverbs 28:26).

So I think "follow your mind, before your heart" is probably a good way to think. Or maybe, it is the way we look at our hearts. Maybe, we have hard hearts, and we should be praying for our hearts to be softened, or changed, or to have a clean heart.

"Create in me a clean heart, oh, God, and renew a right spirit within me" (Psalm 51:10).

I am praying for a clean, softened heart. I want to make the right decisions. I want to do what Jesus would do, and that includes forgiving and trying to hear what the other person might be trying to say. I am praying for understanding and forgiveness of my sins and mistakes. I want to remember not to judge or to hold grudges or to anger too quickly.

"A person who maintains a calm, even temper is quicker to forgive and better able to live peaceably with others" (1 Peter 4:8).

God Never Changes

For everything there is a season, and a time for every purpose under heaven; a time to be born, and a time to die, a time to plant, and a time to pluck up which is planted; a time to kill and a time to heal; a time to break down, and a time to build up; a time to weep, and a time to laugh; a time to mourn, and a time to dance; a time to cast away stones, and a time to gather stones together; a time to embrace, and a time to refrain from embracing; a time to seek, and a time to lose; a time to keep, and a time to cast away; a time to rend, and a time to sew; a time to keep silence, and a time to speak; a time to love, and a time to hate; a time for war, and a time for peace. (Ecclesiastes 3:1–8)

*L*ife is constantly changing. I was in Atlantic, Iowa, the other day and drove by what used to be a Pamida store and now is an implement dealer. I get feed in the old K-Mart store. I drive by the old roller-skating rink that is now Camblin's. Nothing is the same. Anywhere we go, we probably see something that has changed within the last couple of years. Right in this moment, we don't think that things will change or, at least, not change much. But as history has proven, we are wrong.

Nothing is constant. Ever. Not even *we* are constant. None of us stays the same. We are all growing and changing every day. Maybe it isn't as noticeable as when we were infants, and every day, we were learning how to do new things and physically changing very quickly. Now, we are changing and growing inside. Our thoughts and our actions or even our reactions have been evolving and changing our whole lives.

"Jesus Christ is the same yesterday and today and forever" (Hebrews 13:8).

God never changes. He will never be stronger or weaker. His wisdom does not diminish. God doesn't change His values. Uncertainties may shake us, but He is never shaken. God is the rock of all ages, and if we cling to Him, His strength will sustain us.

There are seasons in each of our lives. Sometimes, it's sunny, and sometimes, it is cool and cloudy. Sometimes, it's freezing, and sometimes, it's warm. We have all kinds of factors that will dictate how we will react to certain situations. As we grow and mature, we may handle situations differently. We may grow enough to understand when it is time for a season to be done. When we have outgrown something. And for our own good, we need to let it go and move on.

"When I was a child, I talked like a child, I reasoned like a child. When I became a man, I put the ways of childhood behind me. For now, we see only a reflection as in a mirror. Then, we shall see face-to-face. Now, I know in part; then I shall know fully, even as I am fully known" (1 Corinthians 13:11–12).

So in this season of life, I am clinging to my rock—my Savior. I am letting go of things that may be weighing me down. I have learned that I don't need to hang onto everything. Sometimes, we need to purge. Get rid of what we don't need and make room for new things that will help us grow. Not slow us down or bring us down. We need to be someone that lifts others up and brightens their day. One of my best friends told me today that when I walk in a room, it is like a celebration. Wow, I was speechless. What a beautiful thing to say. She said, in tears, that when I walk in a room, and she is there, she knows that I want to see her, that I want to talk to her. No one could have ever said anything better to me. I truly believe that God is shining through. We have no idea what kind of an impact we may have on someone. Maybe, just maybe, we can be a celebration in other people's lives.

Live Like You Are Dying

Do not boast about tomorrow, for you do
not know what a day may bring.

—Proverbs 27:1

I'm sitting in the living room in my comfy recliner. I am looking out the window; I can see lightning. Hopefully, that means that rain is near. It has been a very stormy spring and summer. We have had hail, wind, rain, and now, it is so dry. It is hard to watch the grass turn brown. Some strong winds ripped through Walnut a while ago. Every street had big, huge trees blown over. It was a mess. We had no idea when we got up that morning how much things would change, pretty much in an instant. We tend to take for granted the things around us—our landscape.

We farm, like a lot of people in this community. The wind from that storm snapped off corn in the fields. It was strange because some of the rows of corn are snapped off, and some rows are fine. But it is a mess and going to be very hard to combine this fall. Farming has changed so much since Mike and I started farming. Farmers have the option to sell "new" crops on the market. So if the price is high, many farmers sell their crops before it is even out of the field. Pretty risky, really.

Most of the time, this works out great, but sometimes, Mother Nature has a different idea. So you sell your crop before it is out of the field expecting a certain amount of yield per acre or an amount of corn that will be harvested. If something would happen like green snap, or hail, or too much rain, or not enough rain, it is not possible to meet that contract that you signed before the crop is out. I was talking to a young farmer after the storm went through, and they were calculating the amount of money that will be "lost." And the first thing that went through my mind was, *But wait a minute, you never HAD that money. You hadn't harvested your crop yet.* We never know what will happen. *Nothing* is promised.

This is true in every aspect of our lives. None of us are promised anything. We aren't promised health, wealth, an easy life. We can't just think that everything is going to be perfect all the time because it isn't going to be. God never promised a perfect life. And He never promised us a certain amount of time on Earth. We go about our lives like we have all the time in the world. We put things off because we can do them tomorrow. Or next week.

There is a very famous song—"Live Like You Are Dying." That goes through my head all the time now. And no, I am not dying. I am healing. I am living every moment to the best of my ability. I am appreciating things and people more than I ever have. I think about things differently now. I feel so strong spiritually and emotionally. It is the strangest thing to explain. I wish everyone had this feeling. It's just too bad that it takes an illness or thinking that our time is limited before we realize we need to make the most of every moment.

"I am sure that neither death nor life, not angels nor rulers, not things present nor things to come nor powers, nor height, nor depth, nor anything else in all creation, will be able to separate us from the love of God in Christ Jesus our Lord" (Romans 8:38–39).

The only thing promised is the love of our Lord, Jesus Christ.

Home Health Nurses Rock!

I know God won't give me anything I can't handle.
I just wish He didn't trust me so much.

—Mother Teresa

*W*e have all heard that a time or two. When someone is going through a rough patch, this phrase is supposed to be comforting. I really don't know why. The truth is, God will give us more than we can handle but not more than He can handle. He wants us to rely on Him in times of trouble.

"Make us rely not on ourselves but on God who raises the dead" (2 Corinthians 1:9).

I'm pretty sure one of the home-health nurses was wondering why God was giving her all she had to go through tonight. I just got my needle put into my port today. I started my second round of infusions. My skin over my port was still pretty swelled up when the nurses were trying to get the needle in the right spot this morning. It took two tries to get it positioned correctly.

They got the dressing on that covers the port and around the port. They have told me repeatedly, if the dressing comes loose at all, call them because there is a big risk of infection if air gets in there. The whole time I had my midline in, the dressing never came loose, and I really didn't baby it at all. I went kayaking and paddle the oar (because someone was just relaxing behind me! Just kidding Kenna). I really didn't let it slow me down.

So today after I got the needle in and did my infusion, I really didn't do anything too strenuous. I actually took a very nice nap in the afternoon. Sweating can make the dressing come loose, and it was pretty hot today, so I really didn't stay outside long, even though Lace and the kids were out there swimming. I like to be out there if anyone is swimming, even if I can't get in.

Later in the afternoon, I looked in the mirror to check on the port and dressing, and I noticed there was a pretty big area that had come loose. I checked a couple times, thinking, *Really? I just got this on today. It has to last a week.* But sure enough, it was loose. I have the phone number of one of my nurses, and we text back-and-forth. She is very quick to respond if I have any questions. So I texted her and told her what was going on. She was at the Iowa State Fair but gave me a number to call. I called the number, and they were going to send someone out.

The nurse on call got a hold of me, and we discussed the situation. She said she had just sat down at a restaurant to eat supper and that it might be a bit before she could get here. She was in Carroll. I said that was fine, I'm in no big hurry. I had stuck a piece of medical tape over the edge of the dressing. A little bit later, she called and said that she had just gone over the interstate bridge coming into Walnut and blew a tire. I felt horrible. First, I interrupt her evening out with her daughter, and then, she blows a tire. I thought, *Man, I really hope I wasn't crying wolf here!* What if she looks at it and says it would have been fine?

She finally got here at 9:45 p.m. She didn't seem too irritated with me after all she had gone through. She looked at the dressing, and sure enough, it was a good thing I called her. She got it all fixed up, and I could already tell a difference on how it felt. It felt a lot better. Then, she said, "After going through all of this, you don't want to have problems!"

I said, "Amen! All is well!" I really did the right thing by calling in.

Better safe than sorry; it is wise to be careful and protect yourself against the risk rather than be careless. That's my motto! And by the way, home health-care nurses *rock*!

Tiny

$\mathcal{L}$ ife on the farm can be kind of tough sometimes. We have had our share of that lately. I had some baby goats born this spring. A set of twins, a set of triplets, another set of twins, and one single. Not too bad for four first-time moms! They were all born without any problems. In the set of triplets, there were two boys and a little, tiny girl. She was so little when she was born! It was hard to imagine that she would survive. But she got right in there with the others to eat and held her own.

My granddaughter, Emery, took a very strong liking to her. She would always go get her out of the pen and hold her and let her run around in the yard. The little goat just didn't grow! She was tiny, hence, the name "Tiny." The last few days, she wasn't looking too chipper, so I would give her medicine. I also tried to bottle feed her.

She never was very interested in the bottle. Her belly seemed full, so I didn't worry too much. Well, this morning, Emery went to check on the goats with a little friend of hers. There was Tiny; she was just lying there, not really moving. Emery jumped in the pen and got her, and I took her to the vet. The vet gave her a couple of shots and some probiotics. He gave her some fluids and then sent her home. I got a bottle ready to try to feed her, and before I could start to feed her, she passed away—basically, in Emery's arms. She was crushed. Her little friend is a farm girl, and she seemed to be knowledgeable in farm animals and farm life. She was trying to comfort Emery; it was so sweet.

Moral of the story is Emery got a little life lesson today. Not a fun one but, unfortunately, part of life. We buried Tiny tonight, and Emery wants to decorate her grave. She was a very loved little goat.

"Blessed are those who mourn, for they will be comforted" (Matthew 5:4).

There is not a right or wrong way to grieve. Everyone grieves differently. If we turn to God, we will find strength and comfort. One of the first stages of grief are shock and denial. Shock is a protective mechanism from being too overwhelmed by the loss. This stage can last a while. I have experienced this with the loss of my sister which was very sudden and unexpected. I have also experienced this with the loss of one of my very good friends last Christmas morning. Even though she had been battling cancer, it was still not something that my mind wanted to accept. She was way too young and had so much to live for, but they are both at peace now and are not suffering anymore.

"He will wipe away every tear from their eyes, and death shall be no more, neither shall there be mourning, nor crying, nor pain anymore, for the former things have passed away" (Revelation 21:4).

Mike said a prayer for Tiny when we put her in the ground. It seemed like the right thing to do. He ended it with, "Someday, we will meet again in heaven."

Until we meet again, Tiny.

Cramming for a Test

It is written, man shall not live by bread alone, but by
every word that comes from the mouth of God.
—Matthew 4:4

I have a very good friend who can cook like no other. She and her husband have three boys who like to eat. Their boys are grown and have families now. They are in a farming operation together, and the head of the operation is at my friend's house. Therefore, she still cooks a lot of meals for them. Even when they are out in the field, harvesting, she will make a five-course meal to take to them to eat in the field which isn't easy! Easy is going to McDonald's drive-thru and taking the guys a sack lunch. But then, the Walnut McDonald's had to go and close! That was a very sad day, indeed!

I was a witness to her awesome cooking again last night. I had helped her set up and serve at her youngest son's wedding rehearsal supper. Of course, she cooked everything herself! Glutton for punishment, if you ask me! But it was all wonderful, and it went very well. I was doing my hosting duties, checking roasters, cleaning up here and there, and someone asked a lady in front of them, "Who made all the food?"

Their reply was that Josh's mom did. She looked at me and asked if I was Josh's mom, and I told her I was not. I sure wish I could have pulled all of this off! I don't think I would even have the guts to try! I don't have enough confidence in myself or my cooking to try to feed over seventy people.

Confidence—I can't say that I have a whole lot of that. I am very leery of doing something wrong, being told I did something wrong, and being embarrassed. I would have to say that one of the areas I am least confident in is knowing the Bible. I was always embarrassed to talk about the Bible or be in Bible studies because I didn't know the Bible very well. I always went to church and taught Sunday school, but I was learning all the way. It has just been in the last few years that I have started to feel more confident in this area. Starting is the key word here. It's a constant work in progress.

"For the Spirit God gave us, does not make us timid, but gives us power, love, and self-discipline" (Proverbs 3:26).

Self-discipline is what I was, and still am, lacking in this area. It was my own fault I felt like I didn't know the Bible very well. I didn't have the self-discipline to take the time to read and study God's Word. I never thought it was really that important. I had my whole life to worry about that! And suddenly, I am fifty-five and facing a very serious illness. Hello! Wake up!

I can honestly say that you guys are witnessing my "cramming" right now. I feel like I am cramming for a test. But I am doing it willingly, not being forced by a parent or teacher. I am feeling the need and desire to learn from God's Word and to read the Scripture. I truly believe that God has put me up to writing this page and for all of you to be able to read it. When I started my Faith and Friends page on Facebook, it was really in a very selfish state of mind. I thought I needed all the support I could get to get through everything that I had coming at me. But what is happening is I am learning from this page and especially from all of you on my Facebook page. Thank you so much!

"Behold, I have put My words in your mouth" (Jeremiah 1:919).

I think we are all in a position to talk about God's Word and to reach as many people as possible. We never know who we might reach or who might reach us in return. And that is what God wants from us. To be disciples. Have a great Sunday!

Second Opinion

But I will hope continually and will praise you yet more and more.
—Psalm 71:14

S o it's finally here. I have been waiting since May 15, 2018, to get into the Mayo Clinic in Rochester, Minnesota. I tried to get in on my own before my diagnosis on May 15 at UNMC in Omaha. I was told there was a very long waiting list. Then, when I was diagnosed, my doctor recommended that I go for a second opinion at the Mayo Clinic. It would be three months before I would be able to get in.

I tried to put it in the back of my mind because I didn't want to wish my whole summer away waiting for August 14 to get here. I think I did well. I kept very busy. May 15, 2018, and August 14, 2018, are etched in my memory forever. And here, I thought the only things embedded in my memory forever were Les Mills Bodypump routines! Oh, and Mossa strength and train releases. And maybe the contemporary Christian songs we sing at contemporary service. I guess I have a better memory than I thought!

But as I have waited, I have never lost hope. I hoped and prayed that the doctors at the Mayo Clinic would stumble across some other diagnosis. Well, maybe not stumble. Maybe with great wisdom and confidence, they will find something that everyone else has missed. I am not going to give up or give in to this diagnosis. I am going to fight like no other. ALS has picked the wrong person to mess with! That's all I'm saying!

"So we do not lose heart. Though our outer self is wasting away, our inner self is being renewed day by day. For this light momentary affliction is preparing for us an eternal weight of glory beyond all comparison, as we look not to the things that are seen but to the things that are unseen. For the things that are seen are transient, but the things that are unseen are eternal" (2 Corinthians 4:16–18).

This light momentary affliction. That is what this is. This is just a moment in my life. These troubles are only making me stronger for my eternal life. I will shed this old imperfect body for a perfect body. One that will last forever. So even though we can't see what is waiting for us, we need to believe that there is something way better than we can even imagine waiting for us. We need to have faith.

"Now faith is the assurance of things hoped for, the conviction of things not seen" (Hebrews 11:1).

So off to the Mayo Clinic I go! I am not looking forward to another EMG, my least favorite test, but if it helps find something else, I will do it with a smile on my face. Which the doctors tell me, most men go out of the room crying after an EMG, and I always smile and laugh. I think because I am basically in shock! And I mean literally in shock!

Please pray some extra prayers for me to have strength, patience, and hope.

This Is the Way

Whether you turn left or to the right, your ears will hear a voice behind you saying, "This is the way, walk in it."
— Isaiah 30:21

I am lucky enough to have an aunt and uncle that live in Rochester, Minnesota. Corky and Brenda graciously offered for us to stay with them while I was going to my appointments at the Mayo Clinic. My aunt also offered to be our navigator, getting us to and from the hospital.

We took off yesterday for my first appointment, and Brenda got us there safe and sound. She knows the inside of Mayo Clinic and Ganda buildings like the back of her hand, so that came in very handy. Piece of cake! We got done with my appointments and headed back home.

So this morning, I had to be back at the hospital by 7:30 a.m. Mike was very confident that he would be able to get us there without Brenda's help. We got out the door in plenty of time so that we wouldn't have to hurry. But things went terribly wrong very, very quickly. Before we knew it, we were outside of Rochester going who knows where! We were so lost! With the help of google maps, we made our way back into town and somehow made it to the hospital. But then, we couldn't find the parking garage entrance. As we were going by one of the hospital entrances, I bailed out of the moving vehicle and ran in the doors. I was thinking, *Man, I hope Mike knows I bailed out!*

Since we had Brenda with us yesterday, I just followed her, and she got me where I needed to be. But as I said earlier, we thought we could handle it. Big mistake! I never paid attention to where we were going. Now, suddenly, I am on my own and have only a couple minutes to spare. But it just happened that when I ran into the building, the elevators were right in front of me. It was even the right building—Gonda Building. That was the building I needed! How did I do that? So I jumped on the elevator, get off on the 8th floor, and amazingly, there was the 8 East Desk right in front of me! I did it!

So we had taken a right instead of a left or left instead of right, but eventually, we made it!

I had a consultation with the doctor again today after the results of my EMG were in. And just so you all know, I will *never* do another EMG again. Never. So next time I say I am going to have an EMG done, remind me that I am not doing that again. Basically, the doctor agreed with the first doctor. ALS. The strange thing about ALS is there is no test for it. It is a process of elimination. Once they rule out every other possibility, they have ALS left. So they say, "I'm very sorry, but the only possible thing it could be is ALS."

So now, I am back to the point of not knowing for sure which way I should turn. I was told that there are stem cell trials that I could possibly be a candidate for. That is something that I have felt all along that I wanted to try and do. You would think it would be a no-brainer. But then, I was told I can't be on the meds that I just started a couple weeks ago before I start the stem cell trial, during it, and for a while after I am done with the trial. Do I want to risk going off my meds for a trial that I don't even know will help me?

"Show me the right path, O Lord; point out the road for me to follow" (Psalm 25:4).

Oreos

I was grocery shopping today and decided I needed to get some cookies. The first kind I see is Oreos. Yum! I love Oreos! My oldest granddaughter doesn't like them. I can't believe that! She obviously doesn't take after her grandma! So I look at all the different kinds of Oreos there are now. Crazy! But what kind do I pick up? Double stuff, of course. I figure if you can have double the yummy goodness, why not? No decision there!

Now, it is time to decide how to eat them. Some people twist them apart and eat the filling in the middle first. Some people just bite into the whole cookie and enjoy the crunchy chocolate and the creamy filling all at once. Some even dunk there Oreo in a glass of milk. That is very tasty as well. There isn't really a wrong way to eat an Oreo. They are good no matter what!

I put the Oreos in my cart and kept moving. As I was shopping, I was thinking how Oreos are a lot like people. There are many different kinds of people, and they do things their own way. We may all think that our way is the right way, but it seems like no matter how you dust, things still get dusted. No matter how you peel a potato, it still gets peeled. Some people peel toward them, and some peel away from them. I peel away, by the way, and that is the best way! Just kidding.

"So we, who are many, are one body in Christ, and individually members one of another" (Romans 12:5).

Even though we all think differently and act differently, we are all children of God. We are all created equally. We are one family of God, and none of us are perfect. We all make mistakes. We are all human. So we really need to remember not to be so quick to judge or criticize others. Respect the ways of others, even if they fold towels differently than you. They still get folded, right?

During the summer, our church goes from two services each Sunday morning to one service. One blended service. Very interesting if you really think about it. Blended. We take a little bit of the contemporary service and a little of the traditional service and blend them. I usually go to the contemporary service because I am in the "Alive in Christ" choir or praise team. We lead the congregation in music. We sing very contemporary songs, most of which you can hear on the radio.

The traditional service sing songs from the hymnal. Very traditional songs. So which service is the right service? Which one is the best service? They both are, of course! There is no wrong way to worship Christ. No wrong way to sing praises.

"What then, brothers? When you come together, each one has a hymn, a lesson, a revelation, a tongue, or an interpretation. Let all things be done for building up" (1 Corinthians 14:26).

No matter how we worship and praise God, sing hymns of anthems, we should do so together—as one. And in life, not put each other down for being different, but build each other up.

Whales

*W*hales. A very large mammal that lives in the ocean. Blue whales are the largest animals that ever lived, even bigger than the largest dinosaurs! Whales have a formal family. Not long ago in the news, there was a story of a mother orca whale that had given birth, and the baby calf had died. She carried that baby on her nose for at least three days. As the dead baby calf fell into the water, the mother would haul it back to the surface. She swam with it for one hundred and fifty miles in the Pacific Ocean. She was mourning her dead baby calf. She wasn't ready to let it go.

Whales also communicate with each other. They are very social creatures. They live in pods and travel together.

For our twenty-fifth wedding anniversary, Mike and I went to Hawaii. It was beautiful. But I have to say, my favorite part of Hawaii were the whales. Yes, my children will attest to this. I believe they grew a little tired of hearing our whale stories when we got back home. We would scan the horizon of the ocean for a glimpse of a whale. We would lie back in the water and float. One day, Mike said, "Hey, I can hear the whales talking!"

I couldn't believe it, so I said, "No way!" and he said, "Yes, I can!" So I decided to try to listen for them too. I lay back in the water just far enough so that my ears were under the water. Sure enough! I could hear the whales talking to each other. It was the most amazing sound. And to think that we were listening in on a whale conversation! It literally took my breath away.

That was definitely my "happy place." I could listen to the whales forever. A year or so later, I had problems with my neck and arm. After many doctors' appointments and tests, one of them being an EMG of course, I just can't get away from those! Anyway, the EMG showed that I had a ruptured disc in my neck. The doctor suggested that I have surgery right away. I agreed just to get out of the constant pain I was in. After all was said and done, I had three discs removed and had three fusions.

After the surgery, I was in my hospital room. I was in some major pain. The nurse said to think of my "happy place." Our friends, Dean and Joy, happened to stop in to see me, and when the nurse suggested to think of a happy place, Dean immediately picked up a piece of chalk and drew a whale on the chalkboard in my room. Now, mind you, he is not a very good artist; I really had to use my imagination to see that it was indeed a whale, but I knew right away what he was drawing. And it made me smile. Actually (that is my grandson's favorite new word right now), to this day, I can still see that drawing in my mind, and it makes me smile and, sometimes, even laugh.

Unshakeable happiness. This is called "joy" or "blessedness" in the Bible. This is happiness that goes deep. Not superficial or shallow. The happiness God wants for us can be ours even in the midst of life's worst pain and sorrow. Or even when we are going through scary times. The best way to have unshakeable happiness is by having fellowship with God.

Blessed are the poor in spirit, for theirs is the kingdom of heaven.

Blessed are they who mourn, for they will be comforted.

Blessed are the meek, for they will inherit the Earth.

Blessed are they who hunger and thirst for righteousness, for they will be satisfied.

Blessed are the merciful, for they will be shown mercy.

Blessed are the clean of heart, for they will see God.

Blessed are the peacemakers, for they will be called children of God.

Blessed are they who are persecuted for the sake of righteousness, for theirs is the kingdom of heaven.

These are the eight beatitudes from the "Sermon on the Mount." Jesus promises us happiness. And true happiness is not just earthly happiness; it is eternal happiness. Heaven.

Pay It Forward

*P*ay it forward. We have all heard that saying before. Random act of kindness. Wouldn't it be nice if we all could remember to do that occasionally? We all get so wrapped up in our own lives, we don't even think about the person behind us at Casey's or the grocery store. Why does it take some tragic event like Molly Tibbets being brutally murdered? Hard to believe in such a quiet Iowa town something like this could happen.

In honor of Molly, two of her friends started a movement. It is called #themollymovement. You can print off little pieces of paper that encourage you to do a random act of kindness. Pay it forward. My daughter found one on her car over the weekend. She paid for the person's lunch behind her in a drive-thru restaurant. She, then, passed the piece of paper on to someone else's windshield. What a wonderful tribute to Molly. And I was also surprised what a small world it is. I know one of Molly's former high school teachers. It is weird how that brings the story of Molly even closer. I know that my friend is grieving and hurting and probably very confused right now.

Another story in the news lately is about a little girl named Sofia. She had cardiomyopathy. It is a condition that can result in heart failure. She needed a heart transplant. Soon. She found out just this week that she was going to get a new heart. She underwent surgery yesterday. She is doing well. Unfortunately, for her to get a new heart, another child had to die. Makes me sad but also happy that the child could help another.

When I had my neck surgery, I needed bone to put in my neck to replace the discs that had ruptured. They used to take bone out of your hip—ouch! I have heard it took longer to heal from that than the actual surgery. I was very blessed to have a bone donor. Someone thought enough about helping others that they became an organ donor. It is a very humbling feeling to think that I have someone else's bone in my neck. But feel so blessed.

"So as those who have been chosen of God, holy and beloved, put on a heart of compassion, kindness, humility, gentleness, and patience" (Colossians 3:12).

God wants and expects us to love one another and help one another. Forgive each other. One of the biggest "acts of kindness" was given by God. He gave His only begotten Son for us! For the forgiveness of our sins. So I would think we could take time out of our life to show a little love and concern for others.

"No man can do me a truer kindness in this world than to pray for me" (Charles Spurgeon).

I think that the world needs tons of prayers. We can do this anytime, every day, for as many people as we wish! There is nothing more powerful than prayer. And it is something that can touch even those we don't know. Just think what the world could be like if we all took time out of our day to just pray and show concern and kindness toward one another.

Longs Peak

I have just returned from a short trip to the Rocky Mountains. We were ten minutes away from Estes Park. We stayed in a very rustic cabin built in the 1940s. The only heat was from the massive fireplace in the living room. The view from the cabin was breathtaking. Gorgeous mountains—Longs Peak, Estes Cone, Twin Sister's Peak. We would sit outside early in the morning and early evening, looking for wildlife to show up. There have been moose, elk, bobcat, and bear sighted right by the cabin in the past. We were really hoping for a sighting of some sort.

When we weren't hanging out at the cabin, we were hiking around on trails, or climbing up mountains, or having a picnic in the Rocky Mountain National Park. The first day, we were done sightseeing and decided to head back to the cabin. As we were driving into town, we drove through an intersection; there was a family of elk standing at the crosswalk, looking back-and-forth, waiting for a safe time to cross. They were looking back-and-forth in unison. We couldn't believe it. So of course, we had to turn around to get a better look. By this time, they had safely crossed the street and were grazing along the side of the road. Tourists were standing close to them taking photos.

The next day, we toured the famous Stanley Hotel. *The Shining* and *Dumb and Dumber* were both filmed there. Come to find out, just the night before, a bear had broken into the hotel and was roaming around. So come to find out, you just need to go into town to see wildlife! Who knew?

In our down time, we would just sit in the rockers outside, facing the mountains. Little chipmunks and ground squirrels were scampering about. We had peanuts that we would feed them. By the end of our stay, they would run up the blankets we had over our laps and, basically, eat out of our hands.

I found a book in the cabin entitled *A Lady's Life in the Rocky Mountains*. It is based on journal entries by Isabella L. Bird. She was a very brave English woman that hiked up Longs Peak just five years after it had first been climbed in 1873. One quote from her book that I found rather ironic is, "One might truly say of the bears, deer, and elk which abound, their tameness is shocking to me."

"You make known to me the path of life; You will fill me with joy in Your presence, with eternal pleasures at Your right hand" (Psalm 16:11).

I just kept looking up at the mountain right in front of me, thinking of that brave, strong woman that traveled over Longs Peak all by herself. Amazing! God chose that path for Isabella Bird. She took it on and followed her dream.

Can I be as brave as Isabella? I hope that I can climb any mountain that God may put in front of me. There is a song that I listen to; "When you don't move the mountains, I'm needing you to move. I will trust, I will trust, I will trust in you." There is that word again—trust.

"In the last days, the mountain of the Lord's temple will be established as the highest mountains; it will be exalted about the hills, and all nations will stream to it" (Isaiah2:2).

No wonder we are so amazed and in awe of the mountains!

Grace

*W*hat a beautiful morning! Since I have started writing this page, many of you have told me how much my posts have helped you or that you are learning from them. Well, believe me, no one is learning more than me. Things have come to me out of nowhere—ideas of what to write about. I notice more things that I never would have before. There have been days when a certain word is in my head all day or a certain song. And I still hear "Grace Got You" every time I get into my vehicle. I woke up to it this morning.

So Mike and I are both in the "Alive in Christ" choir at church. We stand up front with the other members of our choir, and we lead the congregation in music. Mike and I have done a few duets. One of them was the song "Just Be Held" by Casting Crowns. That song means so much to me. We don't need to hold on to God. He is holding on to us. We just need to let Him hold us. The reason I am writing about this is we were doing our weights this morning to music that I choreograph our workouts to. Most of the time, it is contemporary Christian music. There is nothing better to get your day going than to work out to some uplifting music! A little Mandisa can get you going for sure!

So we are doing some exercises to the song "Just Be Held," and one of the verses in the song goes like this, "And not a tear is wasted, in time, you'll understand."

Wow! You know I always listened to the words to this song, and I do remember thinking, *I wonder what that part means?* We got done working out to the song, and it dawned on me; God is holding all our tears in His bottle. That is what this song is talking about.

I knew I had read about that. And it has just been since I started writing these posts on my Faith and Friends page. You may say that you have grown through this page or that it lifts you up when you need it most, but I am growing and being lifted up so much as well. That is God working.

"A sweet friendship refreshes the soul" (Proverbs 27:9).

Thank you, my sweet friends. Have a beautiful day!

"You have kept a record of my wanderings. Put my tears in Your bottle. They are already in Your book. Then, my enemies will retreat when I call You. This I know. God is on my side" (Psalm 56:8–9).

Music

Music is a huge part of my life. It began at a very young age. I can remember when Elvis died. I lived outside of Hancock, Iowa, and my friend Tracy was staying with me for a few days. When we heard that Elvis had passed away, we cried, and in a tribute to him, we sang and danced to his songs. I'm sure that was a beautiful sight!

When I moved to Hancock, I was going into the ninth grade. It didn't take long, and I was involved in band and chorus. I made so many good friends by being involved in music. Not long ago, one of my friends from high school made the comment that her music friends are still the best! I must agree. I'll never forget when our new band instructor came to our school—Mr. Ladwig. Our band was in a very sad state. No one was going out for band. The last instructor we had didn't do our band any justice, to say the least. Mr. Ladwig came to our band program just in the nick of time. He ignited a fire in our little marching band.

Our marching band went from standing on the field at half-time, and I mean standing. We did not move at all and wouldn't have dreamed of memorizing our music. Are you crazy! Well, that all changed quickly when our new instructor showed up. Before long, we were marching around on the field making different formations. And we had our music memorized. We could move about the field in different formations, and we were having a blast. To this day, those are some of the best memories that I have. Yes, I was a band nerd and very proud of it!

I can still remember getting crowned "Spirit of the Band" beside one of my best friends, Kurt Pattee. I was also lucky enough to represent our band at the Clarinda Band Jamboree. It was a very big deal back in the day. It was like representing your 4-H club at the state fair. I am still a band geek. My favorite part of any football game is halftime. I love listening to the marching bands.

We went to Pella, Iowa, to the tulip festival this spring, and they had the most amazing parade with so many awesome high school marching bands. I love the beat of the drums. I really wish I would have been in the drum section! Oh, and another memory I have of band is jazz band. I played the bari sax. I never planned on playing the bari sax. I played the clarinet in marching band and alto clarinet in concert band. Mr. Ladwig took off my shoe, and before I knew it, he put it inside my bari sax.

"It gave it better sound," he said.

Singing is also a very big part of my life. I sang in the choir in high school. I still sing in a choir at our church. About six years ago, a friend of mine and I were making our twice-a-week early-morning trip to the YMCA where we worked out together.

I said to Deb, "Wouldn't it be cool to have a community choir?" I asked another good friend of mine, who happened to be the music instructor at our local school, if she would be interested in directing our little choir. To my delight, Sarah said yes! We had our choir members from our hometown of Walnut and members from Avoca, Shelby, Harlan, Minden, and Oakland. I never dreamed we would have such an amazing group of singers all in one place. The sound is so beautiful. I can't remember for sure when that little vision popped into my head, but it did, and it came to life. We are still doing our Easter Cantata each spring. Once again, I have met so many nice people that I would never have met with out this experience.

So as you can see, music is a very big part of my life. And I don't know where I would be without it. It has helped me get through some pretty tough times. I'm sure we all have songs that take us back to an earlier time in our lives. Some good memories, some bad. But they definitely stir up emotions.

Most of the beautiful music that comes from the Bible comes from Psalms. The word psalms means "to sing, to strike lyre."

"Addressing one another in psalms and hymns and spiritual songs, singing and making melody to the Lord with your heart" (Ephesians 5:19).

"Sing to Him sing praises to Him, tell of all His wondrous works" (Psalm 105:2).

I think the key phrase here is "with all your heart." Do all things in the glory of God and with a pure heart. Sing dance, love, forgive, praise, and never lose faith.

Time

I just sat down and wondered if I had anything I could write about tonight. Nothing was coming to mind, and then, I opened my computer, got onto my Faith and Friends page, and the word "time" popped into my head. So time it is!

Noun; the indefinite continued progress of existence and events in the past, present, and future regarded as a whole.

"Time is the stuff life is made of" (Benjamin Franklin).

Stuff—funny, my aunt just shared a poem entitled "Stuff." My grandma Frannie had written it. When you think about it, we are all obsessed with time. It runs our lives. Time to go to work, time to go to school, time to go to the doctor, time to go on vacation (well that is a good one), time to clean the house, time to mow the yard, and on and on and on. We are always in a hurry it seems. Never enough time. But what is enough time?

Here I am, being faced with the possibility of not having as much time as I thought I might have here on Earth. The average life expectancy is eighty-two point five years for a white woman in Iowa. So I should have a good twenty-seven years of time left. I had a maternal great-grandma that Lived into her nineties. I remember as a young girl, walking up 38th Street with her. She was very tall, if I remember right. But then again, I was only three or four years old. I had a bad habit of sucking my thumb. Must have been pretty bad if I remember doing it! My great-grandma Oakleaf says to me, "Your thumb is going to look like mine if you don't stop sucking your thumb."

I looked at her thumb and thought, *Oh my! I don't want my thumb to look like hers.* It was all wrinkled up and yucky! I don't think

I sucked my thumb again after that! Mission accomplished, Nana Oakleaf! I called her Nana because she would eat a banana every day for breakfast. No wonder she lived to be ninety-four.

On the other hand, her husband, my great grandpa Oakleaf only lived into his mid-sixties. I never knew him. I saw a lot of pictures of him. I remember him being rather tall as well. What happened to me? I missed out on the tall gene!

So why did Grandma get more time than Grandpa? Why do some live well into their eighties and nineties, and some die at infancy or young adulthood. I read a post last night about a beautiful little two-year-old that just found out she has cancer. All over her body. And the young woman, Mollie, whose life was just cut way too short way too soon. I know several young children that have passed away. It doesn't make any sense to me.

"Heaven and Earth will pass away, but my words will never pass away. But about that day or hour, no one knows, not even the angels in heaven, not the Son, but only the Father. Be on guard! Be alert! You do not know when that time will come" (Mark 13:31–33).

So none of us knows how long we have to live on Earth. Not even Jesus knows. But we need to be ready for "the end." Or is it really the end? I know, I'm getting kind of deep here. But the end of time isn't the end at all. Yes, heaven and Earth will pass away, but we will have a new heaven and Earth. How cool will that be?

> Then, I saw a new heaven and a new Earth, for the first heaven and Earth has passed away, and there was no longer any sea. I saw the Holy City, the new Jerusalem, coming down out of heaven from God, prepared as a bride beautifully dressed for her Husband. And I heard a loud voice from the throne saying, "Look, God's dwelling place is now among the people, and He will dwell with them and be their God. He will wipe every tear from their eyes. There will be no more death or mourning or crying or pain, for the old order of things has passed away." (Revelations 21:1–4)

I know since I have been given the diagnosis of ALS, even though I don't have to give in to the prognosis, it has made me appreciate time. I pay more attention to what is going on around me. I take time to really enjoy things. Whether it be the mountains, the weather, the company I am with, my family, being able to watch my grandkids, hold by grandbabies, having lunch with friends, listening to the sermon at church. Time is not guaranteed. It is not a privilege; it is a gift—a very precious gift. We should live our life the best we can, not take it for granted.

I was talking to a friend of mine at an older gentleman's funeral visitation tonight. My friend had been diagnosed with cancer recently. He has gone through chemo and radiation. He was always one to have a big smile on his face, anytime you saw him. It was no different tonight. Even after going through the diagnosis and treatment of cancer, he still had that big smile. He made a comment during our conversation that really hit me hard because I feel the same way. Most of the *stuff* that goes on in our daily lives just doesn't matter. The things that matter, family and friends, are what is important. All the rest of that stuff is not.

So rather than focusing on what can happen or what they say is going to happen to me, I am enjoying every day that I am blessed with. Even if things don't go as I would like. I am going to embrace them. Learn from them. If we look, there are learning moments in each and every day.

Jealousy

$\mathcal{Y}$esterday started like most Sundays for Mike and I; we went to church. Before church, we were visiting with members of the congregation or our church family. There is a friend of ours that always greets everyone with, "Good morning, church family!" followed by, "I love my church family!" She is saying this from her heart.

Mike and I were talking to her and her husband. He was asking me how I was doing and how Mike was doing. He knows that the situation is affecting Mike as well. The gentleman says to me, "You know, I am actually kind of jealous of you, you are going to meet Jesus before me."

It's kind of funny, you would think I would be a little put off by his statement. Like, really? You don't feel sorry for me that I may be dying before any of you? But I knew exactly what he meant, and all I could do was smile.

> It is the same way with the resurrection of the dead. Our earthly bodies are planted in the ground when we die, but they will be raised to live forever. Our bodies are buried in brokenness, but they will be raised in glory. They are buried in weakness, but they will be raised in strength. They are buried as natural human bodies, but they will be raised as spiritual bodies. For just as there are natural bodies, there are also spiritual bodies. (1 Corinthians 15:42–44)

So who wouldn't be excited to get to go to heaven, meet Jesus, be in the presence of our heavenly Father, and get a brand-new body? A perfect body that will never die? Will not be weak or broken? When I really let myself get swallowed up in fear and pity, I just start picturing heaven.

What will heaven be like? What will I do in heaven? Will I recognize loved ones in heaven? Will I know what is going on down on Earth?

"No eye has seen, no ear has heard, no mind has conceived what God has prepared for those who love Him" (1 Corinthians 2:9).

Here are some of the things that the Bible says we will be doing in heaven.

Learning, singing, worshipping, serving, leading, fellowship, and eating. Yay! I love eating! I love singing! I love learning! I love worshipping and fellowship! So basically, we are doing all the things on Earth that we will be doing in heaven. It is like we are preparing for our return home. But in heaven, we won't have sin and guilt and shame weighing us down. It will be wiped away. We will be able to worship and serve the Lord fully and freely.

So no, I don't take offense to that comment. I can understand why this gentleman might be jealous of me. But in the back of my mind, I keep going back to none of us knows when our time is. All we can do is prepare.

Miracles

*Miracles happen every day, change your perception of what
a miracle is, and you'll see them all around you.*
—Jon Bon Jovi

*M*any people have told me that they are praying for me—that they
believe in miracles. That is the sweetest thing anyone could say to me.
How blessed am I to have such powerful believers praying for me?

I had never really thought much about miracles before. I mean,
I know that they are real. I know Jesus made miracles happen all the
time. He turned water in to wine, made the blind see, the deaf to
hear, walked on water.

"Jesus did many other things as well. If every one of them were
written down, I suppose that even the whole world would not have
room for the books that would be written" (John 21:25).

Every day is a miracle. Every day I wake up, and I can get out of
bed and walk is a miracle. I must admit, I used to take it for granted.
I just assumed that I would be able to get up and out of bed and walk
every morning. Now, I know that it is a miracle. Not something to
be taken for granted. And I thank God every night for blessing me
with another beautiful day.

Hearing God is another miracle. And He is working here. I
prayed for so long to be able to "hear" God. And do you know what?
I think I finally realized that I could always hear Him. I just wasn't
listening. Did it take something like being diagnosed with an illness
to get me to listen? Sometimes, God uses situations to get our attention. Hello! He has mine now!

"There are only two ways to live your life. One is as though nothing is a miracle. The other is to live as though everything is a miracle" (Albert Einstein).

I believe that everything in my life is a miracle. God put me right where I am supposed to be with the people I am supposed to be with. So to hear you say, "I believe in miracles," is the sweetest thing anyone could say to me.

> You are Mine for all time; nothing can separate you from My love. Since I have invested My very life in you, be well assured that I will also take care of you. When your mind goes into neutral and your thoughts flow freely, you tend to feel anxious and alone. Your focus becomes problem solving. To get your mind back into gear, just turn toward Me, bringing yourself and your problems into My presence. Many problems vanish instantly in the light of My love, because you realize you are never alone. Other problems may remain, but they become secondary to knowing Me and rejoicing in the relationship I so freely offer you. Each moment you can choose to practice My presence or to practice the presence of problems. (Romans 8:38–39; Exodus 33:14)

I needed this today!

Surrender

*M*att Redman sings a song—"Gracefully Broken." Just like the song says, I think we need to remember that God has got this. God has a plan and knows what my future holds. He will be with me throughout my journey. He will lead me the right way when I decide what medical treatment I may do. There are so many trials out there. It's hard to know what the best one to try is. I think I will wait for my appointment at Mayo Clinic before I decide on anything. I keep feeling like stem cells might be the way to go. So as Matt Redman sings, "Here I am God, arms wide open. Pouring out my life, gracefully broken." I surrender.

Rejoice!

This is the day the Lord hath made, I will rejoice and be glad in it.
—Psalm 118:24

This was the Scripture I read this morning. It is also printed inside the egg cartons that I was filling up with eggs last night. It is one of my favorite Scriptures. One of my good friends' husband recited this Scripture every morning. Even in his battle with cancer, Bob never lost his faith. I pray that I will always be so faithful. Go out and rejoice in this beautiful day!

"Have I not commanded you? Be strong and courageous. Do not be afraid; do not be discouraged, for the Lord your God will be with you wherever you go" (Joshua 1:9).

Noah's Ark

It was by faith that Noah built a large boat to save his family from the flood. He obeyed God, who warned him about things that had never happened before. By his faith, Noah condemned the rest of the world, and he received the righteousness that comes by faith.
—Hebrews 11:7

I have been planning and waiting for this trip to Kentucky to see the "Ark Encounter." All I can say is, "*Wow!*"

It is amazing, almost overwhelming, but so worth coming to see. I would recommend a couple of days, actually, to be able to take it all in. It is quite a sight to see as you pull into the parking lot. Way off in the distance, you see this huge object protruding up from the ground. And as you get closer, it gets bigger, and you finally realize, this is really an exact replica of Noah's Ark. I couldn't imagine all of the trust Noah had in God. He stopped everything he was doing and started to build an ark. People made fun of him, but he kept on persevering. Do I have that much trust and faith in God?

I guess, in the situation I am in, I better? Do I ever feel like I fully trust and put all of my faith in God? Probably not. I still have doubts and fears. But seeing this ark today made me realize that God can make miracles happen.

This morning was my first day trying to give myself my infusions without a nurse standing by, watching me. I felt pretty confident in myself. I had my mom and my aunt close by. I wanted to get the infusion done so we could take off for the ark.

I got all of the medical supplies I needed out and laid them close by so I could reach them all. Almost everything has to be done one-handed. It really has worked out pretty well that I had them put the midline IV in my left arm. When I broke my right wrist a couple of years ago, I had to learn how to do everything left-handed. I am right-handed. So now, this is coming in handy again! Just like riding a horse!

I flush my tubing, no problem. Then, I get the new tubing out of the bag. I begin to prime the line for the first bag of medicine. Going pretty good so far. I get the first bag hooked up, and off we go! I went to breakfast with my rolly pole thingy, or an IV pole as most people like to call it. I got a few funny looks from other people eating their breakfast but nothing too terrible. The first bag ran out in about half an hour, so I went back to my room and started the second bag. Piece of cake!

The second bag is about empty, and I remember thinking that it was so easy to unhook the bag and flush the line again and clip it off. No problem. But this morning, I kind of had a little bit of doubt in myself. What if I do something wrong? What if I forget something? It's kind of important, after all; it is going into my veins! I called my mom and my aunt into my room. They were right next door to us in the hotel. We got everything all flushed and unhooked. So I still needed a little bit of assurance that I was doing things right.

> I have set my rainbow in the clouds, and it will be the sign of the covenant between me and the Earth. Whenever I bring clouds over the Earth and the rainbow appears in the clouds, I will remember My covenant between Me and you and all the living creatures of every kind. Never again will the waters become a flood to destroy all life. Whenever the rainbow appears in the clouds, I will see it and remember the everlasting covenant between God and all living creatures of every kind on Earth. (Genesis 9:3–16)

God gives us assurance every single day. He gives us little reminders that He is with us, and He will never leave us alone. God keeps His promises.

Your Love Never Fails

I am convinced that neither death nor life, neither angels nor demons, neither the present nor the future, nor any powers, neither height nor depth, nor anything else in all creation, will be able to separate us from the love of God that is in Christ Jesus, our Lord.
—Romans 8:38–39

*G*od's love never fails. God's love is eternal. His love goes on and on. I know you will find this hard to believe, but there is a song in my head and has been there all day! I know, I know, very hard to imagine. We had choir practice last night, and we sang this song. I got in my vehicle this morning and, you guessed it, it was on the radio.

"Your love never fails, it never gives up, it never runs out on me. Your love never fails, it never gives up, it never runs out on me. Your love. Because on and on and on and on it goes. Before it overwhelms and satisfies my soul, and I never ever have to be afraid. One thing remains, Your love."

These are some of the lyrics from "One Thing Remains" by Jesus Culture. The phrase that seems to stand out to me at this point and time is, "He never gives up. No matter how bad I mess up, He doesn't leave me. He isn't going to stop loving me, no matter what, His love never fails."

How amazing is that? No matter how bad we mess up, or become so into ourselves that we forget about everyone else, or we fall into the whole gossip thing. Man, that is a bad one! We are all so guilty of it too. Whether we mean to or not, before we know it, we are discussing other people's business, when we don't even know for a fact it's true or not! Weird, I didn't think this was where I was going to go in this post!

It seems like gossip comes up in our sermons at church a lot. Maybe, that means that we have a real problem as a society with it? I know I have tried to become more aware of what I am saying and repeating. How would I feel if the person I was talking about walked up right behind me and heard what we were saying? Would it be hurtful? How would I feel if I were the one that was being gossiped about? Not very good. Nothing can destroy a friendship faster than gossip.

"A troublemaker plants seeds of strife, and a gossip separates the best of friends" (King Solomon).

Mike and I have been watching the show *Big Brother*. It is basically a game of who can outsmart who to win fifty thousand dollars. They will outright lie to each other's faces and play mind games on each other. It is just nuts! I would be a big, old blubbering fool, sitting in the corner. I am not cut out for those kind of mind games.

Unfortunately, this show probably isn't too far away from the truth. So scary! Honesty doesn't hold the same weight as it used to. And we are so worried about fitting in that we will do and say whatever makes us look like we fit in. As I get older—yes, I said it, older—I feel like maybe I am getting a better handle on worrying about what other people think of me. I realize now that the only one that really matters is God. He is the only one that can judge me. No one else has any place judging me. I answer to Him and only Him.

"Let us not become weary in doing good, for at the proper time we will reap a harvest if we do not give up" (Galatians 6:9).

Kind of like gossiping, and the person hears what you are saying, would what you're saying be okay for God to hear? Because He does. He even knows what we are thinking about before we say it. Maybe the old saying, "Think twice before you speak," is a good one to follow?

So just as God never gives up on us, let's not give up on each other. Love one another. We are all in this together.

Friday Night Lights

*F*riday night lights! Gotta love 'em! Our grandson, Korbin, is a senior in high school at AHSTW. He plays on the football team. So what does AHSTW stand for you ask? Well, it stands for Avoca, Hancock, Shelby, Tennant, and Walnut. All small towns in Iowa. With the enrollments going down, the small schools are combining together to make bigger schools. Therefore, we have all of these "alphabet soup" schools. They call them this because of all of the initials in their names.

So this Friday night, AHSTW was playing Westwood. That is another way of naming a school that is combined of many smaller schools. The name of the actual town the football field or school is in isn't actually in the school name. Our daughter-in-law had told me that the game was in Sloan. Since I grew up in Sioux City, I knew it was a little south of there.

Off we go to the game with our friends, Dean and Joy. We figure it will take us an hour and a half or so to get there, so we would have time to stop at a fast-food place to eat. *We* take off in good time and stop in Missouri Valley. Ham and cheese and potato cakes for me please! We stopped at Arby's. We visited for a while and had plenty of time to get to the game. Or so we thought.

Sloan always makes me think of a commercial that was on television when I was growing up in Sioux City. Was it Old Home Bread? There was a trucker, and he had his dog in the truck with him. I can't remember it very well, but it was filmed in Sloan. So I know where Sloan is, just remember that fact!

We drive about thirty minutes. Joy and I are in the back seat, chatting, and pretty soon, we get off an exit. We can see the football field lights not too far away. We are there in good time! We go pay and get a program and walk through the gate. As we were walking through the parking lot, we noticed a bus that said, "West Monona." We continued into the game, and we were discussing the visitor-seating section. It reminded us of Walnut's bleachers that are sitting unused in Walnut, now that we have combined with Avoca.

Joy and I noticed a football team sitting under a big tree off to the left of us. They had on a green-colored uniform. I remember thinking, *Hmmm, you don't see green uniforms very often.* We continue toward the bleachers, and pretty soon, the other team comes running onto the field to the right of us. They are in the color burgundy. Hmmm, AHSTW is blue, white, and red. Maybe the team under the tree is a JV team? AHSTW should be coming out soon. Then, it dawned on Joy and I at the exact same time. We aren't in Kansas anymore Toto! But where are we?

We find Mike and Dean, and we all come to the same conclusion—we are at the wrong game! I was so confused! I asked Mike, "Where are we? We are supposed to be in Sloan!"

Mike's reply was, "No, we are in Onawa!"

I was thinking, *What are we doing in Onawa?*

For some reason on the way up, Mike and Dean decided the game was in Onawa. Too bad, they didn't let the rest of AHSTW know!

I was in the back seat and didn't hear Mike and Dean's conversation about how far it would be to get to Onawa. I had proudly worn my blue-and-red Viking sweatshirt and, after looking around a bit, noticed no one else was wearing red, white, or blue. No Viking attire at all could be seen!

The nice lady at the ticket booth graciously refunded our money but had a very confused look on her face. Understandable. Mike did return the program to her. I was quickly trying to get past everyone in line to get back out of there as fast as possible. I guess we could have said we were "scouting?"

We finally make it back to the pickup, and we all burst out in the loudest, longest laughter I have ever experienced. We could not stop laughing. We headed north a little ways and found Sloan. Of course, there was a very long train that we had to wait for. Why not? We were already late. We made it to the right game, and we even had three minutes left in the first quarter! There were people in red, white, and blue too!

The game was awesome; we won 48–27. Korbin scored three touchdowns and had some amazing blocks. The whole team played very well together. So glad we got to see it!

"I will instruct you and teach you in the way you should go; I will counsel you with My eye upon you" (Psalm 32:8).

It was the strangest feeling, standing there at the football game, not knowing where I was. I knew we were supposed to be in Sloan, but where was our team? Where are our fans? I didn't like that feeling at all! It was awful! That is how we feel if we aren't listening to God and following His path. We feel lost and confused. We need to trust that He knows what is best for us. He knows where we should go. We are so blessed that God does always have His eyes on us. Go Vikings!

Leap of Faith

*T*hat's all I can think of right now. Do I take a huge leap of faith? Sorry, guys, I dragged you all into this with me, but this post is going to be more on the serious side.

When I went to the Mayo Clinic, the doctor gave me the news that she agreed with the doctors at UNMC—ALS. I asked about any stem cell trials that were going on. There is one at Mayo Clinic. I would have to go off of my meds that the nurses and I fought so hard to get on. That really bummed me out. I do feel like the meds are helping me. I feel better when I am taking them, and I don't get as many leg cramps. But if that is the only trial I can get on, I would do it. She also gave me a website to look at. It lists all of the medical trials all over the world. Any kind of trial you can think of.

I have been doing tons of reading for the last year and a half about everything to do with ALS and with medical trials. I had found something about stem cell transplant with cells that have been infused with nerve growth factor. And you can stay on Radicava. Great! Sign me up! But it was in China. And I hadn't been officially diagnosed yet. This was last year. So I have been praying for something like this to become available closer. Be careful what you pray for!

I was cruising that website again last Friday. Looking for anything to do with stem cells. The one showed up at Mayo Clinic again. I had messaged them a while ago, and my doctor at Mayo was supposed to get me info on it but have heard nothing from them. So I keep scrolling through the pages of trials all over the world, and one pops up that looked like something I would be interested in.

I click on it and read, and I was amazed to see that it was stem cells with nerve growth factor infused. It is done at Cedar Sinai in California! I couldn't believe my eyes. I quickly jotted down the information on applying for the trial. I called and left a message. I went outside and wasn't near my phone for a bit. To my surprise, I had already missed a call from California when I got back in the house. I called back and had to leave a message. We played phone tag for a bit, and then, she called back.

She explained the criteria for qualifying for the study. You have to have had symptoms for less than three years; it has to have started in your legs; you have to have breathing capacity of over sixty; you have to be healthy enough to handle major surgery; you have to be able to reside in California for three months. Wow, that is a lot to take in! I asked her right away if I can stay on both of the meds I am on, and she said yes!

I am actually a good candidate as far as I can tell. I had my medical records faxed to her. I have the most awesome group at UNMC. Lisa was right on it when I asked her if she could fax my records; it was done within half an hour. Love them!

I am waiting for a call today to tell me if I am wanted to go out to California to be assessed. They need to run their own tests to see if I am a good candidate. I think I might have seen that they need to test the way my nerves and muscles communicate. EMG. Ugh!

I would be the seventeenth person to have this kind of transplant done. They have two spots left. I have a very good feeling about it, even though it is super scary. So I have been praying, do I take this huge leap of faith? Because as far as I can tell, it would be. It would be a huge test of faith. So many unknowns and things that are out of my comfort zone.

What if I can help further research of this nasty, ugly disease? What if I can help those who are diagnosed in the future? I would sure want that, and I know there have been those ahead of me that have done trials just to help with research. Someone had to take a leap of faith to try Radicava before it was approved.

"But those who hope in the Lord will renew their strength. They will soar on wings like eagles; they will run and not grow weary, they will walk and not be faint" (Isaiah 40:31).

day that the planes were flying into the world trade center buildings." It's been seventeen years. Crazy. Another theory states that between the ages of fifteen and twenty-five, the most formative experiences of our life take place such as our first kiss, first car, first love, and so on. This creates a "reminiscence bump." The farther we move away from that bump, the faster time goes. That seems to make sense.

So no matter how much we would like to, we can't stop time. We can't get in the DeLorean with Michael J. Fox either. Darn it! That would have been awesome! I have no idea where I would want to go, but it would still be cool.

Maybe we are in a season of transition, grief, conflict, illness, unanswered prayers, new challenges, or trying to make a very important decision. We probably wish this "season" would be over all ready! But maybe, it is a season that is a blessing in disguise? Whatever season we are in, we should embrace it. Let it be. The word "amen" means "let it be." Even if we don't love a season we are in, we need to let it be. When our new season comes, we can say amen. We can welcome whatever new season God has in store for us.

I'm having a really hard time trying to decide what my next season will be. Will it be here, or will it be in California doing a stem cell trial? Definitely not a very easy decision. I wish I could fast forward to see which decision I should make or if I made the right one? I'm praying for the direction to take.

One last thing. Since I started writing this tonight, a song keeps popping in my head. My very good friend, Teresa, who passed away on Christmas morning, loved Cher. Loved her to pieces. I can still hear Teresa singing any Cher song that came her way. We would all go out on the dance floor and dance with her as she belted out the lyrics. I can still see her eyes, just as bright as can be, as she sang. We had a blast! So the song that I can hear Teresa sing as I write this is "If I Could Turn Back Time." Miss you!

If God Willing

September 11, 2001. I was doing daycare that morning. I remember a special report coming over the television that caught my attention. A plane had crashed into a World Trade Center building. As the reporters were talking, a picture on the screen was of another plane crashing into the other World Trade Center building. I can remember it like it was yesterday. I remember thinking, *Is this really happening?*

And then, I remember thinking, *We live very close to Offutt Air Force Base in Omaha, Nebraska. Only about sixty miles away. What if that is a target, and they miss?* I had a very uneasy feeling, as did everyone else, that day and for days and weeks to follow. We didn't know what to expect.

Hundreds to thousands of people witnessed this unspeakable crime in person—millions on television. The images were replayed over and over again. It's no wonder many Americans suffer from anxiety disorders. And many of the first responders are suffering from cancer, post-traumatic stress disorder, depression, sleep apnea, and respiratory problems. The toxic dust from the buildings collapsing was still in the air five months later.

> Come now, you who say, "Today or tomorrow we will go to such and such a city and spend a year there and engage in business and make a profit." Yet you do not know what your life will be like tomorrow. You are just a vapor that appears for a little while and then vanishes away. Instead,

you ought to say, "If the Lord wills, we will live and also do this or that." (James 4: 13–15)

None of us expected this to take place. One man, Osama bin Laden changed millions of people's lives that day. The United States has not been the same since. Airport security is very, very strict. Mike found that out the hard way, when we were going through baggage check, and Mike made a joke about having a bomb in his bag. He got told very sternly to not ever say that word again in an airport.

But I also think that all of this did bring our nation together, and our allies were there to support us. It seems like in times of trouble or adversity, people do come together and help each other. I think it also should have made us realize that we have no idea what we will be doing tomorrow or where we will be for that matter.

I can remember a friend's response to the comment, "See you tomorrow!" always was, "If God willing!" How true is that? We don't know what God has planned for us each day when we wake up. We are truly a vapor that is here for just a little moment in time. But we can make the most of the time we do have. God willing.

Breathe

*T*hen He said to me, "Prophesy to these dry bones and say to them, 'Dry bones, hear the word of the Lord! This is what the Sovereign Lord says to these bones, I will make breath enter you, and you will come to life. I will attach tendons to you and make flesh come upon you and cover you with skin. I will put breath in you, and you will come to life. Then, you will know that I am the Lord.'" Ezekiel 37:4-6.

I love working out to Christian music. Really? You might say? But it doesn't have that great beat and catchy lyrics to get you going! Wrong! If any of you have listened to contemporary Christian music lately, you know that it isn't anything like it used to be. One of my favorite artists is Toby Mac. We work out to "Move," "Backseat Driver," and "This Is Not a Test." These are just a few of his songs.

"Move, keep walking, soldier, keep moving on." So basically, this song is saying that no matter what is going on, no matter how bad things get, keep your head up and keep on moving! It isn't over yet; God isn't finished with you. I am trying to live this every day. I am going to keep on living my life. I'm not going to just sit down and give up. God isn't finished yet.

"Backseat Driver." Some of the lyrics are, "You got the wheel, take me where you wanna go. My heart is Yours, no matter where we roll." So this song is saying that we definitely don't want to try to tell God how our life should go. We just need to sit back and roll with it. This is God's road trip! Maybe to California?

"This Is Not a Test." "This is not a, this is not a test, this is the real thing. This is not a, this is not a test. This is the real thing.

We gonna go till we got nothin' left. This is the real thing." So yes, this is the real thing. We only have one shot at living our life as God intended us to. This isn't a practice run!

Another song that we work out to is "Good Morning" by Mandisa. And guess who is featured in this song? Yep! Toby Mac! This is one of my all-time favorite songs to work out to. It gets your blood pumping and your head in the right place. "Good morning! Wake up to a brand-new day. This morning! I'm stepping, I'm stepping, I'm stepping on my way. Good morning! You give me strength, you give me just what I need. And I can feel the hope that's rising up in me. It's a good morning!"

So who wouldn't want to start their day with a little Mandisa and Toby Mac? I have an iPod full of workout songs, and these are my favorites. Waking up and working out to songs full of promise and hope and reminders of who's in the driver's seat. What could be better?

I have a really bad habit. When I listen to the radio, I am always thinking, *Would this be a good song to do Zumba to? Would it be a good song to do biceps to? Or maybe squats?* I listen to songs and try to think what kind of work out I can choreograph to it. So if you meet me going down the highway, and I have my hand up over my head, you might think I am waving at you when, in fact, I am practicing a shoulder routine. Not kidding! Not that I would not wave at you because I totally would!

So once again, I really had no idea what I was going to write about tonight and had no intention on writing about the songs I work out to. But that's what it ended up being! Just goes to show I'm not at the wheel; I'm just sitting here enjoying the ride!

The Scripture that I started with happens to be the inspiration of another song I work out to. It is one that I made into a shoulder workout. "Awake My Soul." I just love the words in this song.

"Breathe on me, breath of God, breathe on me. Breathe on me, breath of God, breathe on me. I come alive, I'm alive when You breathe on me. I come alive, I'm alive, when You breath on me. Awake, awake, awake my soul, God, resurrect these bones. From death to life to You alone, awake my soul."

God's Word breathes life in us. It can resurrect our soul and bring life to our dry old bones. It is kind of cool to be working out to these songs. Talking about breathing new life in us and waking up to a good morning. No matter how tired I am or how much I really don't feel like working out, I know I need to keep moving. After all, this is not a test; this is the real thing!

Bells

A hand bell choir or ensemble is a group that rings recognizable music with melodies and harmony. Our church, Trinity Lutheran Church, in Avoca, Iowa, has a bell choir. My daughter, Lacey, and I both joined several years ago. Probably more years ago than I remember. When we joined the group, our bell choir went from two octaves to three octaves. We each play three or four bells. I play in the bass clef which is kind of strange for me because I sing soprano. I have never looked at the bass clef before.

Lacey and I play at the very end of the line. The biggest bells. The bells are set up on a long table. They are arranged in the order of the keys on the piano which doesn't help me at all because I never learned how to play the piano. Although, I can play a mean Chopsticks! There are ten of us lined up that play bells. Plus, we have our director. Before we start to practice, we have to get our bells out. While we are getting our bells out and getting ready to play, there are several conversations going on at one time. Since Lacey and I are at one end of the table, we really can't hear what that they are talking about at the other end.

Tonight, I was chatting with the gal on the one side of me, and in the distance, I hear, "When a guy is massaging your legs, and he looks you right in the eye!"

I thought, *What in the world is going on down there on the other end of the table? I want in on that conversation!* So I stuck my head back so I could see who was talking, and she looked at me and smiled. What do you think they were talking about? I assumed she was getting a massage but, in fact, she was talking about getting a pedicure. We all got a good laugh out of the whole thing.

It made me think about how rumors get started. Down on our end of the table, we only heard part of the conversation. And right away, we come to our own conclusion. Judy had gotten a massage. But when I inquired about what she was talking about, it was a pedicure. Granted, most of the time you do get your legs massaged with a pedicure, but that's beside the point.

> You shall make the robe of the ephod all of blue. It shall have an opening for the head in the middle of it, with a woven binding around the opening, like the opening in a garment, so that it may not tear. On its hem you shall make pomegranates of blue and purple and scarlet yarns, around it's hem, with bells of gold between them, a golden bell and a pomegranate, around the hem of the robe. And it shall be on Aaron when he ministers, and its sound shall be heard when he goes into the Holy Place before the Lord, and when he comes out, so that he does not die. (Exodus 28:31–35)

The sound of the little bells ringing while the priest moved around was the sound of him being alive—being accepted by God. If the ringing stopped, it meant God had rejected him, and he was dead. So when the people of God heard ringing bells, it was a good thing. So when we ring our gold bells, which are super shiny right now because we just waxed them, it should remind us of the good news, that now we can all be accepted by God and we can all be made alive in Him because of what our Great High Priest, Jesus Christ did on our behalf.

"Look, Daddy, teacher says every time a bell rings, an angel gets her wings." I think everyone knows what movie this famous line was in. *It's a Wonderful Life*. George Bailey was contemplating suicide. Prayers for George reached heaven, and Clarence Odbody, angel second class, was assigned to save George. In return, he will earn his wings. Prayers reached heaven, and George was saved. That is an awesome image, isn't it? Just goes to show how powerful prayers are!

"Behold, I send an angel before thee, to keep thee in the way, and to bring thee into the place which I have prepared" (Exodus 23:20).

I think it is very comforting to think that I have a guardian angel. A messenger from God. I wonder if I will be able to be in a bell choir in heaven? That will be some beautiful music!

My Rock

*T*oday was kind of crazy. I got up at 4:30 a.m. to exercise. I had to be in Omaha by 8:00 a.m. for the ALS clinic. I actually made it with three minutes to spare! Then, I went to Hy-Vee in Council Bluffs to pick up food for driver's appreciation week. I was planning on making food for it today but didn't get that to fit into the schedule. Thanks, Hy-Vee! Then, I came home and did some of the usual chores around the house. At about 2:00 p.m., I hit the wall.

I had been going full steam ahead and bam! My body said, "We are done!" It was kind of a roller coaster today. First thing this morning, I'm sitting smack dab next to a gentleman that was farther along in this disease than me. Granted, I have been around a couple of people with it, but at that time, I never dreamed I would be in the same boat.

This man looked so sad. He didn't make eye contact. He didn't have any facial expressions. He did have someone with him. She didn't visit either. It was a very sad situation. I almost felt guilty because I was able to walk in there, look at my phone, fill out paperwork; I am capable of doing pretty much whatever I need to do.

I wanted to talk to him but didn't get the impression he wanted to talk. So I just sat there and looked at my phone. I kept thinking, *Man, I hope people don't feel like they can't talk to me if I am ever in that situation. I don't want to be ignored.*

Just having my needle in my port makes people avoid eye contact. Funny, why do we do that? I know I'm just as guilty. Just because someone is in a wheelchair or has braces on their legs or a neck brace on, we shy away from them. We don't make eye contact.

My name is called, and I go back into the room to have the physical therapist, speech therapist, respiratory therapist, social worker, nutritionist, and Dr. Thai all come in and run their tests on me. So I can still make the "zzz" sound forever! The actual comment was, "Very impressive!" This is a test to see how your mouth and throat muscles are doing. I can do all kinds of cognitive skills; I weigh the exact same as I did the last time I was there—to the ounce! How did I do that? They want me to stay at the weight I am. They don't want me to lose weight. So when she asks what I have been eating, and I say potato chips, she doesn't get mad!

Dr. Thai came in to do his clinical tests. It was interesting to me that he didn't check my reflexes. I think he knows they are very brisk! But he did check the strength in my right leg. I hold my knee up off of the chair I am sitting on. He pushes down on the top of my knee, and I'm supposed to keep it from going down. The last year or so, when he pushed down on it, I couldn't keep it from going down. Today, he pushed on it, and I actually held it up a little longer. It felt like it was stronger, but I wasn't sure. But Dr. Thai said that he thought it seemed stronger too. So it wasn't my imagination!

I talked to my Radicava nurse today too. All she does is work for Radicava. That is the brand-new drug I am taking by infusion. If I have any questions or problems with the medication, she is the one I talk to. That is her job. She has been trying to come see me. She is from Illinois, but it just hasn't worked out. She asked how I was doing, and I told her that I think my leg feels a little stronger, and I don't get as many cramps when I am on the drug. She was thrilled but reminded me it isn't a cure; it just slows the progression down. Bam! Back down to reality again. She did seem very interested knowing that I am having some positive responses. This drug is so new, and everyone is so different. She is learning from us.

Dr. Thai and I discussed the trial in California. He is very much a supporter of medical trials. He just wants me to ask lots of questions when I go talk to them next week. He said some of the anti-rejection medications are very close to chemo. That got my attention. I really don't want to waste the good days I have right now being sick from the medicine I have to take for a year. So I will keep doing my own research and wait until I actually talk to the people in California, before I make my final decision on if I will do the stem cell transplant.

"For God alone my soul waits in silence; from Him comes my salvation. He alone is my rock and my salvation, my fortress; I shall not be greatly shaken" (Psalm 62:1–2).

Hurricanes

Katrina, Sandy, Harvey, Isaac, Beryl, Maria, Florence, Irene, Ernesto, Nate, Jose, Wilma, Ophelia, Isabel, Rita, Gordon. Are these the most popular baby names of all time? No, you got it, these are names of past hurricanes. How do they come up with the names of hurricanes you ask? Well, hurricane names are chosen by the World Meteorological Organization. The Atlantic is assigned six lists of names with one list used each year. Every sixth year, the list begins again. The very first hurricane of the year will start with the letter *A*, the next *B*, and so on. The letters *Q, U, X, Y,* and *Z* are not used. If a hurricane was extremely destructive, its name is retired and never used again. Since 1954, forty names have been retired.

"For you have been a defense for the helpless. A defense for the needy in his distress, a refuge from the storm, a shade from the heat; for the breath of the ruthless is like a rain storm against a wall" (Isaiah 25:4).

The storms of life. We all have them. Some seem like hurricanes, others are just sprinkles on and off again. But none of us can say that we go through life with perfectly sunny days all of the time. Wouldn't that be awesome? Or would it?

God reminds us over and over again that in this world, life won't be a bed of roses. We are going to have hard times and sadness, and grief and hurt. But God is always right there with us, and we are never the same person when we walk out of a storm than when we walked into it. Have you ever thought about that? Has there ever been a very difficult time in your life, and you just wanted it to be done? It was too much to handle? But when you finally stepped out of the storm, you were changed? You were stronger, more confident, had more compassion?

Looking back at some of the worst times in my life, I can honestly see how I grew from that experience or gained life-changing knowledge. It's what we take away from that experience that is important. And we have to remember that God never promised us that life would be easy, but He does promise that He is bigger than any storm we will face, and He is always working for our good.

"He caused the storm to be still so that the waves of the sea were hushed" (Psalm 107:29).

During this storm in my life, I am clinging to God. I am trusting that He is testing me and having me go through all of this for some sort of good. I am getting ready to make one of the biggest decisions I think I have ever had to make. Do I get a stem cell transplant? Do I put myself through a five-hour surgery which is just a trial? Not a guarantee of instant healing but possibly a longer, better quality of life. I will be quite frank; I think the thing that bothers me the most is not the five-hour surgery, or the recuperation period, or taking the anti-rejection meds. It's being away from my family for three months. I really can't wrap that thought around in my head. I live within two miles of all my kids and grandkids. I know, how blessed am I?

The other thing is, I will miss Halloween, Thanksgiving, and Christmas with my family at home, along with many other events that take place this time of year. But I guess I have to look at the big picture. Maybe this time away for three months could give me three more years than I would have had.

My mom has been amazing through all of this. I will call or text her and say, "Hey, Mom, check this trial out," or "Look this treatment up," and she is a trooper and digs right in! She has been very strong. There was one time when she let her guard down a little. She was trying not to cry, and she said to me, "You are my rock through this, you have been so strong."

I guess I feel like I am doing what I need to do. Mom also made the comment that she is worried about this decision that I am trying to make. I told her, "Don't start worrying yet. Let's wait until after I have gone to talk to them about the trial and have done my testing to see if they even want me." I need to take one day at a time. I feel like God is leading me in a certain direction. I am kind of trying to step off to the edge of the path, but He keeps leading me back.

"In the eye of the storm, You remain in control. And in the middle of the war, You guard my soul. You alone are the anchor, when my sails are torn. Your love surrounds me, in the eye of the storm." These are lyrics from "Eye of the Storm" by Ryan Stevenson.

I love this faith-filled perspective, I'm going to let God's love wrap around me and shelter me during this storm, not from this storm. There is a difference.

You Say

"*Y*ou say I am loved when I can't feel a thing. You say I am strong when I think I am weak. You say I am held when I am falling short. When I don't belong, You say I am yours."

These are the lyrics from a song by Lauren Daigle—"You Say." I was listening to the radio in my vehicle the other day, and this song came on. I had to take a second glance at the station my radio was tuned to. I had turned it to 98.5 for a bit. It surprised me when "You Say" came on because it is a contemporary Christian song that is very popular right now on Christian radio stations. I wasn't listening to a Christian radio station at that moment. It was a rock station.

I was surprised, but it was a happy surprise. This song has crossed over to the rock stations. Awesome! Maybe, it will touch people that would have never heard that music before.

"The only thing that matters now is everything You think of me. In You I find my worth, in You I find my identity." These are more lyrics from the song.

God loves us even if we can't feel it; when we feel weak, He makes us strong. This is so true. It is at the time we feel the weakest, yet we keep going, that God is holding us and making us strong again. I have felt that so much throughout this journey. Sometimes, I wonder how in the world am I going to handle this? The obvious explanation is God is holding me up.

"Fear not, for I am with you; be not dismayed, for I am your God; I will strengthen you, I will help you, I will uphold you with My righteous right hand" (Isaiah 41:10).

Persevere

A few years ago, we were down in the Ozarks with some friends. There are tons of ledges and cliffs around the edge of the lake. For some reason, a few of us decided to jump off one of the ledges into the water. Brittney, Korbin, and I jumped off. I hadn't done anything like that before. When I jumped off, I got this feeling in the pit of my stomach like it was going to jump out of my throat! I remember looking down and thinking, *That is a LONG way down there*, and without realizing it, I curled up into the fetal position. I finally, after what seemed like hours, hit the water. And I mean hit hard. My thigh took the brunt of the landing, and I remember going under water and letting out a very loud scream! Of course, no one could hear me, but I still felt better!

When I finally surfaced again, everyone in our pontoon boat that was watching were all laughing. I'm like, really? I could be dying here, but they said that they could hear the clap of when my leg and, I have to be honest, my butt hit the water. They knew how painful it must have been. So I climb out of the water, walk up the rocky bank of the lake, and up the side of the ledge. Yep, I am going again. I have to prove to myself that I can do it without curling up into the fetal position. So I jumped again, and I did manage to keep my legs straight down, so my feet hit the water first. Much, much better. Then, if I remember right, I did it one more time for good measure. I had a huge bruise on my thigh and butt for a good two months. It was black for quite a while.

I have talked about going to El Salvador on a mission trip several times. We worked in the mornings while it was cool, then, we would do other things in the afternoons. One day, we handed out little Crocs (shoes) to families, we toured around the area, and one day, we played "football" with the local kids. So their football is like our soccer. I never played soccer, but I ended up coaching when my kids were playing. So I did learn a lot about the game.

We, the missionaries, played against the local children. And let me tell you, they take it seriously and are very good. Some of them would have been high school age. So we start the game, and I find out they don't care that I'm a white woman who is over fifty and only five feet two inches. They showed no mercy on me. I ended up flat on my back several times. If I stood my ground, they literally ran over me and never looked back. It was so cute though, the littlest boys on the team, they had to be around six or seven years old, came over and took my hands and pulled me up.

I never really thought of myself as being competitive, but I am. I don't feel like I have to be better than the competitors; I am competitive for myself. I want to do something until I get it right or to prove to myself that I can do it. I remember coming off the soccer field, bleeding, and thinking, *Who is this person? Where did she come from?* I didn't even go out for sports in high school. Probably a good thing because I might have gotten kicked out of the games!

I think now, though, that this trait I have in me is carrying me. The feeling of, I am not quitting till I get it right—I am not giving in—is coming in very handy right now. Yes, I do get up every morning and very gingerly get out of bed just in case my leg decides to give out on me. But I don't just lie in bed just in case my leg might not work, although it is very tempting sometimes!

"Blessed is the one who perseveres under trial because, having stood the test, that person will receive the crown of life that the Lord has promised to those who love Him" (James 1:12).

It would be very easy to let myself fall away from God right now. To be angry with Him that I have this disease and there is no cure. I could just jump off my rock and give in. But authentic faith deals with trials by clinging to Christ. If we bail out when things get rough, then, we never really had a true faith.

I know, as I have gone through life, there have been times when I didn't know if my faith was enough. This is one situation that I would have thought I would be freaking out and panicking, but I, most days, have felt a very strong sense of peace. God has this handled if I just hang on and trust Him. So I am clinging to Him and my faith.

Beverly Hillbillies

*W*ell, we made it to Beverly Hills! Just call us the Clampetts! Wow, do we feel way out of our comfort zone. We were starving by the time we made it to our hotel room and thought we would just go to the restaurant that is attached to the hotel. We walked in and felt very underdressed. We sat down and looked at the menu. We couldn't find any prices. We hightailed it out of there! After flying for three hours, driving for two, we just wanted a burger and fries. We walked a couple blocks and found a "Fatburger." That hit the spot!

Tomorrow, I have tests from nine o'clock to three o'clock. I will meet with one of the doctors first thing, so I will be able to ask questions. Hopefully, I will think of everything I should ask. We do have a list, but we probably forgot something.

I know you are all praying for me. I guess what I need are prayers for guidance of if I should be doing this study or not.

"Let me hear your lovingkindness in the morning; for I trust in You; teach me the way in which I should walk; for to You I lift up my soul" (Psalm 143:8).

Bloom Where You Are Planted

No, my daughter. It's not My time for you.
Bloom where you are planted.

—1 Corinthians 7:20

*M*ike and I flew to Los Angeles on Wednesday. We took a shuttle from the airport to our hotel that is two blocks from Cedars Sinai. It has turned out to be the best location for us. We can walk to the hospital and to the restaurants nearby.

The first night, we decided to eat at the restaurant attached to the hotel. Remember we took off before we really gave it a chance? We ended up going back there last night and had some appetizers. It is a Mediterranean restaurant. You know what? I really liked it!

I have to admit I was a little out of my comfort zone staying in this neighborhood. West Hollywood. But we have only been here a couple days, and I already feel more at home. Well, that might be a little strong, but I feel more comfortable. The people around here are so diverse and so friendly. Yes, there is the occasional homeless person standing around which makes me so sad. You can tell they are just lost souls. We went to a couple of different beaches today, and there were homeless people camped out all over. They had all of their belongings right by them. Many of them were still sleeping on the beach while people were walking around them. What a sad, sad life.

There is a reason I have been pulled to California. Yes, I was very uncomfortable at first, but I quickly became more at ease. I took the time to really look around and take the surroundings in—to notice and appreciate all of the cultures in this one area. From the shuttle driver, to the five Uber drivers we had, to the doctors and nurses and coordinators at Cedars Sinai.

I still don't know if I have been approved for the study. I did tests all day yesterday, but some of the results will take a few days. It is still so hard to decide if I want to uproot myself and come out here for three months. During my favorite time of year, no less. But if it will give me more time or help someone in the future with ALS, I guess I could plant myself here for three months. I am pretty sure I would be able to come home for Thanksgiving and Christmas. Bonus!

Bloom where you are planted. God is telling us we can grow and flourish wherever we are. Sometimes, it's in the places we feel the most uncomfortable that we learn the most.

Big Girl Pants

*G*et your big girl pants on! This morning, when I woke up, the first thing that popped into my head was, *What am I going to do? I need to make a decision!* And the reply I heard in my head was, *Get your big girl pants on!* Would God really say that to me?

I wondered if maybe He was trying to get my attention in more ways than one? Not just in this decision that I am going to have to make really soon, but in my spiritual life as well?

"Lay aside immaturity, and live and walk in the way of insight" (Proverbs 9:6).

When we are babies, we are completely dependent on our parents. As we grow up, we become more independent. But if you think about it, our spiritual journeys are just the opposite. We start out thinking we know it all and don't need God. Then, we finally start to realize, hey, I do need God! I can't do this all by myself! At least, that is how my journey has gone.

It seems that as we "grow" in faith, we want to learn more and more. And we don't just wait until Sunday morning to hear the message—not that we shouldn't go and listen to the message on Sunday morning, don't get me wrong. But we are digging deeper into the Bible all on our own.

We are all teaching each other. Teaching the Gospel is an expectation for all Christians. Just by talking about the Bible, repeating Scriptures, and helping others hear and learn about the Bible. We are all doing that! We are teaching each other and growing spiritually as a result.

"All Scripture is God-breathed and is useful for teaching, rebuking, correcting, and training in righteousness, so that the man of God may be thoroughly equipped for every good work" (2 Timothy 3:16–17).

So maybe, God was telling me to get my big girl pants on for a couple of reasons. First, I think He is telling me that I need to keep growing and maturing in my faith. If I keep growing spiritually, then any decision I need to make will be so much easier. It will be made in the confidence of knowing that I have faith in God that He will guide me in the right direction.

I go to bed at night and pray, "Please let me hear Your voice." This morning, I heard it loud and clear. "Get your big girl pants on!"

Knock

Ask and it will be given to you; seek and you will find;
knock and the door will be opened to you.
—Matthew 7:7

*A*sk. The first thing we do when we need help or guidance is to pray. I have been praying for some sort of treatment or trial for me to do for quite a while now. I have asked for guidance on the direction I should take over and over again.

"Pray without ceasing" (1 Thessalonians 5:17).

God wants us to continually talk to Him. That keeps our relationship with Him strong.

Seek. We should always actively seek out God. We need to focus on Him and do it with our whole heart. We can look for God anywhere. At church, at home, in the park, driving down the road. We can see Him in our children, our parents, and our grandkids. Everywhere we look, God is there. The mountains, rainbows, the ocean, fresh snow.

So I prayed and prayed, and I found a stem cell trial. I think God was saying, "Here ya go!" Next, I seek out the trial. I contacted the neurology department at Cedars Sinai.

They said, "Come out to California, we need to run some tests to see if you would be a good candidate."

It took a lot of faith to jump on a plane and go to California for something I didn't even know if I will qualify for, or even want to pursue. But Mike and I jumped on a plane!

Knock. I definitely am knocking on the door now. It is so close. I have asked, and I have sought, and now, I have knocked. I am praying that this door I have been actively seeking is opened. But God will open it in His time. Not mine. So I am still waiting for that door to open.

I do know, however, that if this door does not open, it is because it isn't the right door. I have done what I believe God has lead me to do, so now, I have to wait and see if the time is right.

"When one door closes, another opens; but we often look so long and so regretfully upon the closed door that we do not see the one which has opened for us" (Alexander Graham Bell).

I also have faith that God will guide me down the right path to the door that will open.

YMCA

I went to the YMCA today to visit with my friends from the class I used to instruct. *Used* to is the day word here. I delivered some shirts to them and sat and watched as they worked out. Man, that was tough!

I sat and thought about how much weight I used to lift, how many reps we did, how many push-ups we did. As hard as it was, I loved it. Now, I am lucky if I can do a few push-ups. Planks, I can last a little while, but nothing like I used to. I remember doing planks before and thinking, *I wonder how long I can hold this?* I felt like I could hold that position forever.

It was awesome to see everyone. I have seen a few of them off and on. But good to see the group. After class, I sat and visited with a couple of the gals. During the course of our conversation, one of them made the comment, "We can't compare what we used to do, to what we can do now." How true is that?

None of us are the same now as we were even last year—physically, mentally, spiritually. We are changing all the time. In some ways, we are growing—hopefully, anyway—in our mind and in our spiritual lives. But in some ways, we are failing just a little bit, but it's all a part of the aging process.

I was watching the *Today Show*, and they were talking about "super-agers." These are individuals that live well into their eighties, nineties, and hundreds. They are fit as a fiddle. Well, their body is as fit as could be expected. There is a study that is being done, and they are following these super-agers. And when they die, they donate their brains to science. It is the best way to study the difference between their brains and "normal-aging" brains.

They have found that in the super-agers, there is a special motor neuron. It is called "economo" neurons. Sign me up! Super-agers have four to five times as many of these in their brains. Forty percent of these super-agers actually have no symptoms of dementia in life, but after they die, they have full-fledged signs of Alzheimer's disease in their brains.

So it really makes me wonder why do some people have "extra-special" neurons and live till they are one hundred, and some of us have unhealthy neurons that die early? Hmmm. I think I have more research to do! It just proves that the human body is very complex, and none of us are the same. It also proves to me that they are getting closer and closer to figuring out these neurological puzzles. That is why we have to be able to do what we can while we can to help further research. Part of the process of the study I am considering is they follow me the rest of my life. I would check in every six months, and I would agree to an autopsy after my death. No problem, it makes total sense to me.

"Do not say, 'Why were the old days better than these?' For it is not wise to ask such questions" (Ecclesiastes 7:10).

My life might not be the same as it was a year ago, but you know what? I think it is better! My relationships, my outlook, my determination, my relationship with God. Life is good.

I just found out that the door I was knocking on did not open. I guess God has a different door for me! Keep on praying for the right one to open. May God bless you all!

About the Author

*L*esley is a fifty-six-year-old mother of three and grandmother of nine. She and her husband, Mike, run a farming operation and a trucking agency in Iowa. She is very active in her community and her church. She loves to exercise and leads classes several days a week. But things started to change in January of 2017. Things began to feel heavier, and her balance was not as good as it used to be. Lesley also began to have extreme fatigue which was not like her at all.

By August of 2017, she noticed the muscles in her thigh twitching. The strange part about that is she could see them but couldn't feel them. Since she had a neurology appointment coming up soon, she decided to wait and talk to her neurologist about it. Let the testing begin.

This is the story of Lesley's journey to get a diagnosis so that she knew what she was up against and to decide what treatments would be best, if any. As a way of letting friends and family know the latest test results, she started a closed group on Facebook, not realizing that she was touching the lives of those who were reading her page. She started the page as a form of support for herself during this frightening journey, and to her surprise, people started telling her how much she was inspiring them. The small closed group grew and grew. Friends started adding friends. People would ask to join. God was at work. He is definitely working through her. None of this was planned, at least not by Lesley. But she feels the need to write now which she never did before this journey. She found that writing out her experiences and trials helps her through this journey. She was diagnosed with ALS on May 15, 2018. Her motto quickly began, #fightlikeagirl. And she does!